Foundations of Grant Writing
A systemic approach based on experience

Hill M. Walker, Ph.D.
Center on Human Development
College of Education

Sari M. Pascoe, Ph.D.
Office of Innovation Program Services

Kindle Direct Publishing. You can purchase more copies of this book at Amazon.com

Library of Congress Cataloging-in-Publication Data
Foundations of Grant Writing.
A systemic approach based on experience.
Hill M. Walker, Ph.D. and Sari M. Pascoe, Ph.D.

p. cm.
1. Grant writing. 2. Grant writing foundations. 3. Fundraising.
4. Funding sources. 5. Writing principles. 6. Grant proposals.
7. Grant writer. 8. Grantsmanship.

ISBN 978-0-9839120-5-7

Printed in the United States of America

University of Oregon
Innovation Partnership Services
1238 University of Oregon
Eugene, OR. 97403-1238

Dedication

To those whose initial efforts are rejected but who persevere and use the feedback to develop a better proposal.

– Hill Walker –

To dreamers and doers alike who want to bring about change to their communities and need a little help in doing so through grant writing.

– Sari Pascoe –

Acknowledgements

This book derived from a grant-writing module developed by Hill M. Walker, Ph.D. and published by the University of Oregon, entitled: Preparing Fundable Grant Proposals (2012). We wish to express our appreciation to the Association of University Centers in Disabilities and the Center on Human Development at the University of Oregon for their support of the development, publication and dissemination of the parent version of this book.

At the University of Oregon, Rob Horner, Ph.D., his graduate students, and selected faculty made important evaluative comments regarding changes to the parent version of this manuscript that were most useful in the revision and editing processes of this book. We appreciate greatly their feedback and efforts. We also thank Mike Bullis, Ph.D. for his generous contribution to this publication.

We appreciate the support received from the Innovation Partnership Services (IPS) office at the University of Oregon. Under the leadership of Charles Williams, Ph.D., J.D., the IPS office collaborated with us from concept to publication and supported our efforts along the way. We would also like to recognize the contribution of Daniel Pascoe Aguilar, Ph.D. (reader), Kevin Maness, Ph.D. (reader), Michael Wells, CFRE (reader), David Frazee Johnson (resource), Leslie Martinez (resource), Jeff Geiger (resource), and the Marketing Communications office at the University of Oregon (print design) for their valuable contributions to this publication.

Foreword

I am honored to have been asked to write the foreword for this book on the intricacies of the grant writing process. As a grant writer for almost 30-years who has been awarded more than $23 million of grants and contracts, I can attest to the truth of the statement on page 11 of the book that grant writing is, in fact, an "art." Let me quickly add that there is absolutely no question that to be successful in the grant writing process one must be facile with the subject in question. Conversely, there also is absolutely no question that to be successful one must write a proposal that presents the required information powerfully, clearly, in the correct order, and within the page limit set for a given competition.

Over the course of my career engaged in grant writing as a research faculty living on "soft" (grant) money, as a tenured faculty member building a scholarly profile, and as the former dean of the College of Education at the University of Oregon reviewing our faculty members' widespread and highly successful grant activities, I have been astounded at the nuances of grantsmanship. The winners in the grant process are not always the best-informed or best scholars; often those who prevail in a grant competition are those who are able to package their ideas in an understandable and convincing way – something that too many faculty in higher education and administrators and staff of non-profit agencies simply don't know how to do effectively.

This is an essential reference for potential grant writers, and even for seasoned grant writers. Given the vagaries of the grant process, the lack of preparation presented by many, and frustrations many experience when faced with writing a proposal, this book addresses a critical hole in the skill sets of many in higher education and in agencies. Those who carefully read and reflect on the strategies presented in this book will have a considerable advantage over peers who do not possess the wisdom and "tricks" described in the following pages.

There simply are no better tutors from whom to learn grant-writing skills than Dr. Hill Walker and Dr. Sari Pascoe. I have known Hill as a graduate student, colleague, and close friend for more than 30-years. In fact, I took a course on grant writing from Hill in my early years as a doctoral student and I attribute much of my success in academia to his instruction and guidance.

I also have worked closely with Sari in her role within the University of Oregon focusing on intellectual property issues. I have always found her to be organized, clear, and enjoyable – qualities that shine through in the narrative. Together they form a powerful duo, as Hill is an expert on governmental grant competitions and Sari an expert on grant writing in the private sector. The fact this book addresses both public and private segments of the grant writing world is unique and important.

I strongly believe that the pages you read herein will unlock the mysteries of the grant process. I wish you good luck.

Michael Bullis, Ph.D.
Sommerville-Knight Professor
Department of Educational Methodology, Policy, & Leadership
College of Education, University of Oregon

Table of Contents

Table of Figures

Chapter I
Introduction

Background and Overview

From birth, most of us are exposed to and impacted by storytelling from our peers and from the adults we learn from and interact with. For some, storytelling has a central role in preserving culture and customs, just like early humans did long before biblical times. Storytelling also has a central role to play in the contexts of fundraising and the grants procurement process. It allows funders and agency staff to gain a mental picture of how their values and missions can mesh with priorities that drive positive and sometimes innovative change(s) across communities. This principle operates similarly within and across foundational, corporate and public funding contexts where priorities are identified and grant applications are procured and awarded to effect change. This procurement process has been in existence at least since the time of ancient Egypt, where there are records of grants being awarded by the Pharaohs to achieve specific goals.

The primary calling of the grant writer is to engage in strategic storytelling to paint a picture that can be understood by many--yet resonate with the few who can make a difference. The grant writer's duty is to serve as the liaison between those in need and those having the resources to close gaps in needed funding for action and important outcomes.

This book is designed with the novice grant writer in mind so as to enable improvements in their grant writing skills. It seeks to enhance the skills of professionals and graduate students who compete for federal grants. Individuals having no or only limited experience with the grant writing process are most likely to benefit from the content of this book. By improving your grant writing skills, you can increase your success rate as a professional and contribute to making a difference in your community context.

Foundations of Grant Writing is the result of a collaboration between Hill Walker, Ph.D. and Sari Pascoe, Ph.D. both of the University of Oregon. The original inspiration for this current work stemmed from Hill's creation and publication of a self-directed, multimedia instructional module designed for individuals with no experience or limited prior experience (mostly graduate students and young professionals) in seeking competitively awarded funding from federal and state agencies in the fields of education, developmental disabilities, mental health, community psychology, and human and social services. This module, published in 2012, included instructional materials for understanding key concepts and applying skills whose mastery is essential for successful grant writing. Preparing Fundable Grant Proposals (2012[1]) was jointly published in 2012 by the University of Oregon (UO) Office of Innovation Partnership Services and by the National Association of University Centers on Disabilities. This module was distributed to more than 70 programs of the National Network of University Centers for Excellence in Developmental Disabilities that were affiliated with the Association of University Centers on Disabilities. It was also distributed to the national Network of 43 LEND[2] programs.

In Foundations of Grant Writing we saw an opportunity to make the core concepts, established principles, and proven strategies of this module available to a wider audience of professionals interested in pursuing grant writing in order to access funding from corporate foundations, NGOs, and state and federal sources. An advantage of this current book is that, unlike Preparing Fundable Proposals, its content addresses grant writing in both public and private sectors and should thus appeal to a more diverse audience.

Purpose and Goals

Today, grant writing has expanded from being a practice to a highly specialized professional field. In this book, we focus on recommended strategies for critical decision-making during the grant writing process rather than focusing solely on the mechanics of the practice. The goal of this book is to improve your performance as a professional and to help you develop confidence as a grant writer in order to better compete in your field or area of expertise (see Figure 1). Specific outcomes targeted for the book are:

a) to enhance your knowledge and skills when competing for available funding by describing and reviewing concepts fundamental to successful grant writing

b) to promote your immediate implementation of developed skills by making experiential and tacit knowledge explicit and compelling

[1] Walker, H. (2012). Preparing Fundable Grant Proposals: A Roadmap for Professionals. Eugene, OR: UO
[2] LEND – Leadership Education in Neurodevelopmental and related Disabilities programs

c) to inform you of available pathways for grant writing by exploring potential funding sources and their identities

d) to enhance your grant writing capacity by furthering your understanding of this specialized field so you can become a change agent in your community.

Figure 1. Goal and Purposes

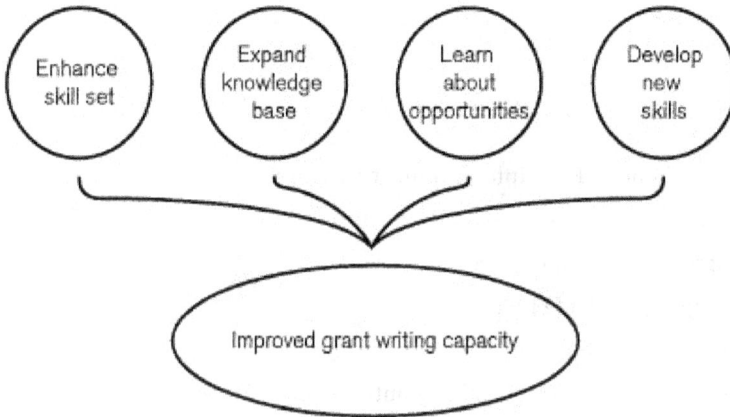

This book is designed for you as a career professional who may be new to the grant writing process including interns and graduate students. We assume that if you are reading this book it is because a) you are interested in becoming an experienced grant writer, and/or b) you have had sufficient experience with writing proposals to know that you need help. We designed this book with you in mind.

We understand grant writing to be an art form of sorts —as a method of strategic storytelling that takes time to develop. We know that the more experience you have in grant writing, as a general rule, the better you are at it. Thus, by developing and strengthening your skills and by being persistent while working on your craft, the odds are reasonable that you can secure success as a grant writer (as measured by either the amount of money raised and/or by the number of proposals funded). Whatever way you choose to measure your success, it is important that you define your identity and capacity as a grant writer to better match the expectations of those you represent whether yourself or an organization.

In the grant writing module developed by Walker (2012), Preparing Fundable Grant Proposals, core elements that should be addressed in the grant writing process are described. These elements are listed below and divided into two parts. Part 1 describes the generic strategies and critical issues that account for success in effective grant writing. Part 2 provides the means for making a compelling argument for your proposal and what you plan to do should you be funded. In the remainder of this book, we attempt to distill and abstract for you the most important takeaway lessons from this material. For readers who wish to access a more detailed and comprehensive explication of grant writing strategies, please contact the National Association of Centers for Disabilities to access a copy of the original grant writing module (Preparing Fundable Grant Proposals) (AUCD contact information: 1100 Wayne Ave. #100, Silver Spring, MD, 20910/ 301-588-8252).

The Core Elements of Effective Grant Writing

Part 1:   Generic Principles, Strategies and Issues in Successful Grant Writing

1.1 Learning the grant writing process

1.1 Background and experience

1.1 Developing fundable ideas

1.1 Basic process used to develop grant proposals

1.1 Principles of being an effective grants person

1.1 Use of graphics to summarize and integrate large bodies of information

1.1 Importance of words, rules, language fluency, and images in grant writing

1.1 Understanding how peer review panels work

1.1 Collaborating with others

Part 2: Making a Compelling Case or Argument for Your Proposal

1.1 Overview of the case argument process

1.1 Parallels in journalism (syndicated columnists) and the legal profession (trial lawyers)

1.1 Approaches to making an effective case

1.1 Key concepts and vocabulary to use in building the case argument (e.g., schemata, heuristic, metaphor, etc.)

1.1 Making the case convincingly (argumentative writing)

1.1 The role of major and minor premises

1.1 Use of available literature, observations, logical analysis and assumptions as premises to support claims

1.1 Writing the case argument from an ordered set of premises

1.1 Deductive and inductive forms of logic and their use in grant writing

1.1 Anticipating the reviewer's criticisms, questions and potential biases

This book explores the foundations of grant writing in four additional chapters, starting by recognizing grant writing as an art form and identifying basic principles in chapter two. In chapter three, the foundations of grant writing are examined by developing an understanding of these key principles and the profile of the grant writer, in addition to the study of structure and details through the development process. An analysis of the identity and dynamics of funding sources is the content focus of chapter four. In chapter five, an overview of the foundations of grant writing is provided with a description and review of core grant-writing concepts, principles and strategies that were presented throughout the book.

We designed this book to provide a systemic understanding of the field of grant writing, focusing on the competition for funding. We decided to provide charts and illustrations to complement the content presented, yet not include actual proposal samples although reviewing both funded and non-funded grant proposals is a very good idea. You can learn a tremendous amount from this exercise, particularly if you can obtain reviewers' comments associated with the grant applications you are able to review. Since they are public documents, the funding agency may be able to supply you with copies of applications and reviews if you make such a request. Failing that, you next option would be to contact the author(s) of the grant about such a request.

It is important to note that the grants process involves three critically important phases: 1) competing for funding, 2) managing funded projects effectively, and 3) reporting and disseminating outcomes. This book addresses issues pertaining primarily to phase one of this process. However, to have a success within this specialization, you must acquire essential knowledge in phases two and three.

About the Authors

Hill Walker –

I have been involved in competing for federal grants since the late 1960s.During this ensuing period, together with my colleagues, I have accounted for over $40 million in competitively awarded federal grants to support a continuing series of demonstration, model development, personnel preparation, program development, and research applications through the University of Oregon (UO) and the Oregon Research Institute I have participated in all phases of the grant development and grant review processes associated with the development, procurement, and review of federal grants. I originated and taught the tool subject course in grant writing and project management over a 13-

year period at the UO and continue to serve as a mentor to both younger faculty and graduate students in the grant writing process.

I have always been interested in improving a diversity of human relationship challenges (e.g., youth violence prevention; school safety; antisocial behavior in school age children; childhood behavior disorders) through action and research. That is how I began my grant-writing career. I became educated about the grant-writing process to the best of my abilities through my graduate training. The ability to write compelling grant applications that address important priorities has been perhaps the most important career development achievement I have experienced.

Sari Pascoe –

I have been a grant writer for more than 15 years, not always as a professional placement (e.g., consultant), yet always complementing my performance on the job (e.g., executive administrator for nonprofits). I have had the opportunity to serve on proposal review panels and funding decision-making committees, and to design and write a diversity of proposals that have been fully awarded. My professional career has expanded to higher education, nonprofit, K-12, government, and research institutions across the U.S. and Latin America. This has allowed me to enrich my grant writing, project management, and reporting skill set. As a grant writer for higher education and nonprofit institutions, I learned promptly that networking and collaboration are key elements that could define my success. By working diligently in improving my skill set, as well as consistently developing and strengthening relationships through transparent communication, I was able to develop a robust portfolio of awarded proposals. I have presented to grant writers, and continue to be invited to consult with grant writers who are developing their skills sets as professionals.

I was born in Mexico City and went to college there. I have lived in the U.S.A. for more than two decades. I earned my Ph.D. from Indiana University in Bloomington with a focus on systemic transformation of organizations. I had the opportunity to work full time and study at night for about 15 years. During this time, my professional placements evolved from teaching in, to researching about, to administering organizations. I enjoyed very much applying in the work place what I learned in the classroom and vice versa. My academic and professional development has been closely related to educational and youth serving environments. I enjoyed collaborating on this book because I believe that by harnessing these fundamental skills you can cause positive change in your community and beyond. Today I collaborate with the University of Oregon, working

6

with faculty innovators and the intellectual property issues that result from their innovations. I am also CEO of my consulting firm, providing strategic planning and solutions for teams and businesses. You can find more information about me at Linkedin: www.linkedin.com/in/sydpascoe 2008.

The content of this book is informed by the results of our collective, four decades of experience as grant writers. We are hopeful that the material herein makes your task of securing grant funding easier and more likely.

Chapter II
Grant Writing as an Art Form

We argue herein that grant writing is an art form. Throughout this book you will see this construct recurrently as represented in the form of meaningful story telling through the grant writing process. Meaningful story telling is learned. Our view is that the skill sets necessary to compete successfully for grants and/or secure a successful grant-writing career can be learned and improved upon over time by almost anyone who applies him or herself to the task.

Successful grant writing is a technical skill that can be learned by most. We estimate that this complex skill set will be more easily mastered by some than others —this is especially the case for those with well-developed language skills, who can think logically and clearly, and who have mastered a range of methodologies for investigating important questions and problems. By learning the grant-writing process through systematic study, careful observation, reflective analysis, and participation in key skill-development activities, you can secure a successful career as a grant writer (see Figure 2). There are many ways to develop your grant writing skills.

A good way to begin developing relevant knowledge about grant writing is to attend either a university-level class or a custom-designed workshop about the topic (these usually offer certificates of completion[3]). If you do not have access to these opportunities (e.g., availability, expense), there are numerous published materials on grant writing in the form of books, manuals, tip sheets, and fee-based grant-writing workshops that are offered periodically on a regional or state-level

By learning the grant writing process through systematic study, careful observation, reflective analysis, and participation in key skill-development activities you can secure a successful career as a grant writer

At the center of your development efforts should be collegial networking

---

[3] GPA – Grants Professionals Association™ – Certification Institute (http://grantprofessionals.org/professional-development/gpc-credential)

basis. As a rule, these materials require considerable adaptation to one's situation and professional interests.

Serving on peer-review panels affords you the opportunity to experience first-hand the workings of its operation, response patterns, and decision-making structures for funding allocation

At the center of your development efforts should be collegial networking. By establishing ongoing communication with professionals, scheduling potential shadowing opportunities, setting up informational interviews, and nurturing collaborative prospects, you may advance your knowledge about grant writing exponentially. Your networking should be complemented with participation, if possible, in reviewing successfully funded grant applications and participating/ volunteering in review committees.

By accessing examples of funded grant proposals, you will be able to start identifying patterns of key information, style, and messaging across proposals. You might also be able to access reviewers' feedback. This is instrumental in better understanding what makes a grant proposal successful —or not. Serving on peer-review grant panels is another learning experience, affording you the opportunity to witness first-hand the workings of a review panel's operation, the dynamics of panel members during peer review deliberations, and the decision-making structures used for

Learn from successful grant writers

funding allocations. This experience will allow you to observe directly the dynamics of peer-review panel operations and is especially revealing of how individual reviewer biases can shape the panel's decision in positive or negative ways. There is really no substitute for directly observing this process and, in so doing, learning how to anticipate and pre-correct for such biases in your own proposals.

Affiliating with and volunteering your time and effort with successful professional grant writers can be another effective way of learning about the grant writing process. This depends upon how deeply the lead investigator is willing to involve you in the proposal development process and how open the process is. Some investigators are rather protective in this situation, which obviously limits its value. This option generally works best when you can join a team of researchers who are proven, successful grant writers. One avenue for developing solid experience in writing grants within professional settings is local nonprofits.

These agencies are usually interested in increasing their income generation capacity with grant writing being one key strategy to meet or supplement their annual budget requirements. Hence, it could be important to meet Executive or Development Directors of nonprofits in your community. You can initially secure an opportunity to develop skills as an unpaid intern. Eventually, as proposals are awarded, you can earn an hourly income as a consultant or staff member. This could prove to be an efficient and effective way to develop your grant-writing skills (and contribute to your community's development and quality of life). It is important to point out that your best opportunity to learn would be from a successful grant writer who is willing to mentor you through the grant-writing exercise. Both of us personally took the time to mentor up-and-coming grant writers some of whom are now accomplished grant writers leading nonprofits, in academia, or in public industry sectors.

It is our recommendation that you find ways to develop a systemic understanding of the grant-writing field, from diverse perspectives, and access opportunities to experience first-hand the challenges that come with submitting successful and unsuccessful proposals, as well as participating in reviewing them. Discovering the reasons why you were or were not funded is a powerful way to achieve this goal.

For those readers who are expanding their academic careers, some funding agencies, such as many of those within the National Institutes of Health (NIH), have a program of funding for new or junior investigators. In such programs, the eligibility requirements are generally that a) you must be within seven years of having received your doctorate and b) you cannot have been previously funded. In this way, the playing field is made more level, and new investigators are competing against each other rather than against the full range of expertise represented by all applicants. If this option is available to you, we highly recommend that you consider it carefully.

Many grant applications are rejected, in part, because review panels do not believe the lead applicant has the necessary skills, knowledge, and experience to be successful

Finally, an apprenticeship model exists in many fields where individuals can apply for post-doctoral fellowships. In doing so, they can learn a whole range of skills relating to the research process and competing successfully for grants at a federal level. In the fields of psychology and education, there have traditionally been exemplary post-doctoral opportunities available at some major research universities as well as within established institutes and centers. A number of outstanding scholar-researchers have developed their grant-writing skills within these programs.

Regarding federally funded grants, your background and experience, as related to the area(s) in which you are developing a grant, are of paramount importance in determining a successful outcome. Over half of all grant applications are rejected in part because review panels do not believe the lead applicant has the necessary skills, knowledge, and experience to conduct the project successfully. This poses an obvious barrier for individuals early in their professional careers who do not yet have the necessary credentials. It also highlights the importance of publishing in one's selected areas of expertise and participating in experiences that can be highlighted as valuable and relevant in building a case for your content knowledge or technical skills. These are two areas that are looked at very carefully by review panels in judging an applicant's competence and fundability.

Figure 2. Strategies for developing a systemic understanding of grant writing

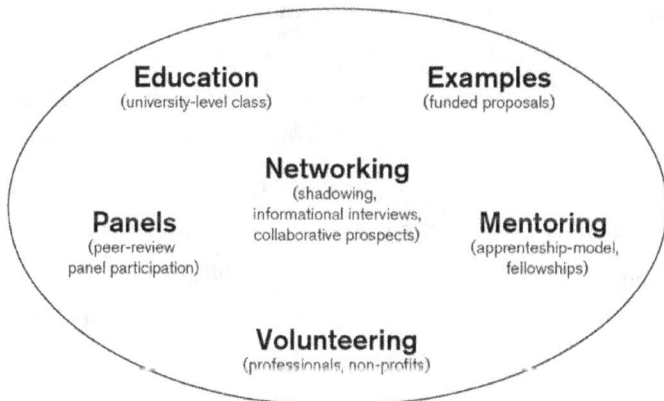

Education
(university-level class)

Examples
(funded proposals)

Networking
(shadowing, informational interviews, collaborative prospects)

Panels
(peer-review panel participation)

Mentoring
(apprenteship-model, fellowships)

Volunteering
(professionals, non-profits)

S.M.P., 2014

The content of this book addresses both private and federal/state funding opportunities and sources. We provide a systemic understanding of the field of grant writing and the current funding landscape. We highlight many of the differences between collaborating with private versus public funding sources. Yet, you will find that for purposes of your grant writing application, the required skill set, experience, and challenges will be very similar.

Basic Principles: A Systemic Approach

This chapter offers a bird's-eye-view appraisal of the core concepts that comprise successful grant-writing proposals, including their development from ideation to submission, the use of language and visuals, and mastering the grant writing process. By gaining an overall understanding of these basic principles, we hope that you will better understand the infrastructure necessary to successfully develop a proposal from the initial design to the final award decision.

Developing Proposals

Developing a grant application from beginning to end is a generic process that subsumes a number of important tasks, such as selecting a topic or focus for the grant, developing a schema, and building a compelling case argument that may be relevant to most types of grants. We have used a basic, sequential process over the years to frame grant applications.

As a general rule, especially if you are in an academic setting, you should select an interest area within your career focus domain(s) —that is, one in which you are committed to doing long-term work. If you are not in an academic setting, consider establishing a meaningful affiliation with an organization that holds similar values and views to yours. This decision could help ensure that your passion and commitment drive your grant-writing process and that you have the wherewithal to pursue it. As you search for researchable topics, priorities, and ideas within this area, we recommend that whenever possible you develop a list of pro and con arguments or reasons for either pursuing the topic or not. Carefully considering the tradeoffs that exist among capacity, costs, benefits, importance, personal motivation, and the time and effort involved in

There are some funding agencies (both public and private) that almost never fund an application on the first submission so your willingness to stay with the cycle (i.e., develop, submit, meet rejection, revise, resubmit) becomes a very important issue. It may be helpful to note that for some federal funding sources, the first submission rarely even gets reviewed —that is, it is judged to be unscoreable. One should not be discouraged by this outcome and become so disheartened as to give up. On the contrary, use it as a valuable experience to inform the content and decision process for other grant proposals.

Personal motivation and capacity to carry out the work are two important dimensions to consider as a grant writer

Your estimate of the likelihood of being funded is another important consideration. You must consider whether you are able to accurately gauge your *personal motivation* (or your client/ institution's commitment) and capacity to carry out the work. These are probably the two most important dimensions to consider in your decision to apply for a grant (see Figure 3). It is also important to remember that by submitting a grant proposal, you may be writing your job description for the next one to five years. So, what you propose to do in the application should be achievable given current circumstances. Reaching consensus when grant writing for clients on 1) which grant proposals to submit and 2) the scope of work assumed should the grant proposal(s) be awarded is important. Some of these tasks require careful negotiation on your part as they can directly affect your work and quality of life. Some funding agencies allow numerous resubmissions of the same application or iterations of it. However, most others have limits on how many times this can occur. This would be important information to have before the initial submission of a grant. For example, private funding agencies will allow you to submit a proposal for funding of the same project after a period has elapsed from the time when the original submission was declined (one or more years).

Figure 3. Decision to write a grant

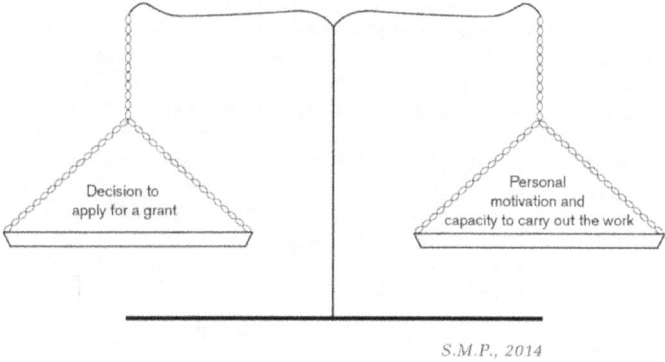

S.M.P., 2014

Having thorough knowledge of the content area(s) in which you are competing can be central to your success as a grant writer

After selecting an interest area and identifying a researchable topic, a next important step is to assess the general landscape and status of the topic you have chosen. Generally, one is expected to review the last 10 or 15 years of research literature on the selected topic to use this information to characterize the topic's current status, and to buttress the need for additional work on it. Individual donors and local foundations will expect you to be knowledgeable about current conditions in the socio-cultural-economic landscape of your community, as well as about the impact in the community caused by your institution. This review can be especially helpful in developing a plan to define and frame the topic, to identify influencing factors, to present your model or approach to solving a

problem or addressing the topical focus of the grant, and to predicting outcomes likely to result from the work, if funded. Such strategic planning can be invaluable in making a convincing case argument, as skilled grant writers often use this information in the *background* and *significance* sections of the grant application.

Having thorough knowledge of the content area(s) in which you are competing can be central to your success as a grant writer. The greater your mastery in this regard, the more likely it is you will be successful in your efforts to secure funding through grant writing. It is extremely important that, as a professional, you are sensitive to emerging trends in your area(s) of expertise. Review panels are most impressed with proposals that document such trends and then design cost-effective, researchable solutions to address them. You can only do this if you are able to a) read extensively, deeply, and carefully in relevant areas of literature, b) become aware of new federal legislation and policies relating to such trends, and c) understand the critical issues that influence practices based upon them.

Thus, staying on top of critically important problems within your field (i.e., ones in which society has a vested interest in seeing solved) is of paramount importance! As a general rule, if the public is very concerned about systematically addressing specific topics/issues, public interest in them is likely to be sustained for years into the future. This is true for both public and private funding opportunities. Importantly, how you make your knowledge explicit can sometimes be the difference in securing funding. Your capacity to engage the funder's interest in written form becomes paramount and is an example of the relevance of becoming an effective and strategic storyteller. President Bill Clinton has famously said it this way: "the best story wins."

Public interest in specific topics could result in sustainable funding

We recommend the use of a problem-solving approach in determining researchable priorities. By that we mean a high priority problem is identified and a researchable solution(s) is developed for it, which can be investigated through a funded application. We address this concept in depth in the next chapter. Over the years, we have found this problem-solution oriented approach to be highly effective in developing researchable ideas and review panels have generally responded well to them. Another approach, implemented by a range of research universities, focuses primarily on the method of investigating a problem. That is, the investigative method is of equal or sometimes greater research interest than the problem being studied, which, in some cases, may not be broadly recognized as one of critical importance.

It is likely that the research ecologies at other institutions are based on a mix of these two approaches. This is not to suggest that one approach is superior to the other, but that identifying a critically important problem or priority and then designing a solution to it provides a useful structure for a grant —especially early on in one's professional career. In perhaps a majority of cases, the federal Requests for Proposals (RFPs) process used to procure grant applications is seeking solutions to important problems or priorities. New legislation, and the mandated policies that flow from it, nearly always create numerous instances in which novel fundable ideas and priorities emerge. In conducting a conceptual analysis of emerging knowledge bases on priority topics, you should thoroughly review existing and past attempts at responding to these challenges and know what their limitations are before attempting to build a case for a new or different approach. In so doing, *you must try to show that the allocation of a federal/private grant to your proposed research or approach is a better investment of funds than what currently exists or has been tried in the past.*

Finally, focus on building grant applications around assessment or intervention programs that are well researched. If these are promising or proven in terms of their evidence base, they are likely to appeal to practitioners and researchers. Collaborating with higher education institutions (i.e., research universities) could result in the development of products funded by awarded grants. All of these products enhance the professional capacity and effectiveness of field-based professionals and result in better decision-making and delivery of services and supports. These products, and ones like them, have the status they do because they have been extensively researched and numerous publications have been developed around them which can be cited to build the case for their further development in grant applications.

Proficient Grant Writing

Use language with fluency, persuasion, and creativity

Perhaps one of the most essential factors in accounting for the achievements of successful grant writers is their ability to use language with fluency, persuasion, and creativity. Embedded in this principle is also the ability to think logically. Applicants who can combine these attributes effectively have a colossal advantage in the grant writing process (see Figure 4).

Figure 4. Critical attributes of the successful grant writer

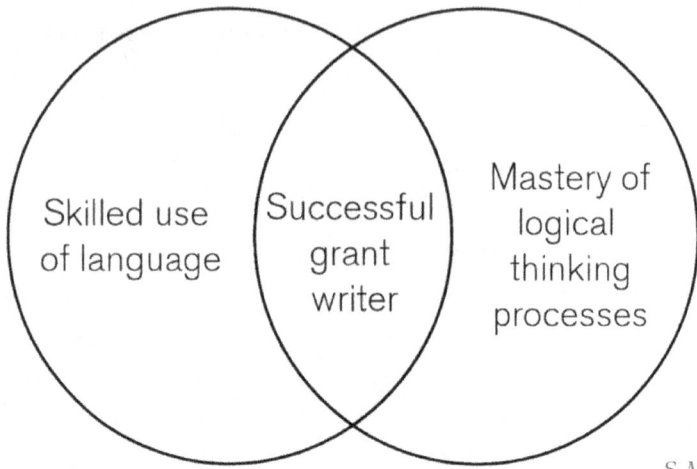

Skilled use of language — Successful grant writer — Mastery of logical thinking processes

S.M.P., 2014

There are certain key skills and psychosocial attributes that comprise the profile of an effective grant writer. However, considerable variation in these attributes exists across effective grant writers. Mistakes and errors that inevitably occur in a proposal should be viewed as learning and skill development opportunities rather than as simple reviewer bias, systemic or bureaucratic error, and/or unjustified rejection of the application — unless, that is, you have incontrovertible evidence that such is the case! Two lessons flowing from this principle are that 1) you will learn far more from your grant writing errors and mistakes than from any successes you may have and 2) the best way to avoid having these weaknesses pointed out to you is to anticipate and pre-correct for them. Ideally, it is much better for you to point out potential weaknesses or liabilities in your approach, and design remedies for them, than it is to assume this risk and hope that reviewers will not detect them. When that happens, the damage to the prospects for your proposal can be substantial and quite difficult to offset and recover from within the application.

You are likely to learn far more from your grant writing errors and mistakes than from any successes you may have

Psychosocial attributes affect both novice and expert grant writers. In this context, for example, Hill has found that his irritability index goes up considerably when he is fully engaged in the grant writing-development process. It is something he has struggled to control over the years, but usually without success. Once, when Hill was so engaged, his then 13-year old son came into the house and saw him working at his computer with books and journals spread all over. When he discovered that Hill was writing another grant, he said he was leaving home! It was a shock for Hill to realize how much impact this process could have on family members and associates. For Sari, the grant writing process usually affects her ability to balance work and wellness. Once, after receiving awards for each and all of her proposed grants submitted within a one-year period, her health system became compromised and she landed in the hospital for two weeks with pneumonia.

The grant writing process is difficult and rigorous, yet it can also be very rewarding

The grant writing process is difficult and rigorous, requiring considerable sacrifice on some occasions. This process can also be very rewarding when at the end of the funder's decision-making process your grant proposal is approved for funding. In our careers, there have been occasions when grants were due right after major holidays. Accepting responsibility to lead the grant-writing process through these periods usually has a direct impact on every member of the family, including oneself. Frequently, there is a period of doubt for many grant writers as to whether the outcomes and products promised in the grant can actually be delivered. This speaks to the wisdom of building in a planning year to major grants whenever possible. Further, if, at some point, it seems likely that promised deliverables may not be forthcoming, one may have the option of renegotiating them with the funding agency or project officer early on in the project.

There are selected principles and strategies that we regard as the "DNA" of a successful grant writing and development effort. These have been derived through lessons learned from our participation in diverse phases of the grant writing process. These include: a) having a lead role in developing grant applications, b) evaluating reviewers' comments and feedback on grants submitted, c) serving on review panels that appraised a diverse array of grants and grant types, d) serving on site review teams to help facilitate pending grant decisions, as well as on site evaluation teams to review progress with a previously funded grant, and e) participating with colleagues in an advisory capacity to assist federal agencies in drafting legislation, reviewing policy, and establishing potential funding priorities (see Figure 5). All other things being equal, we believe those who can absorb these lessons and apply them systematically are advantaged over others in the grant-competition process.

Figure 5. Valuable skill-building experiences in becoming a more knowledgeable grant writer

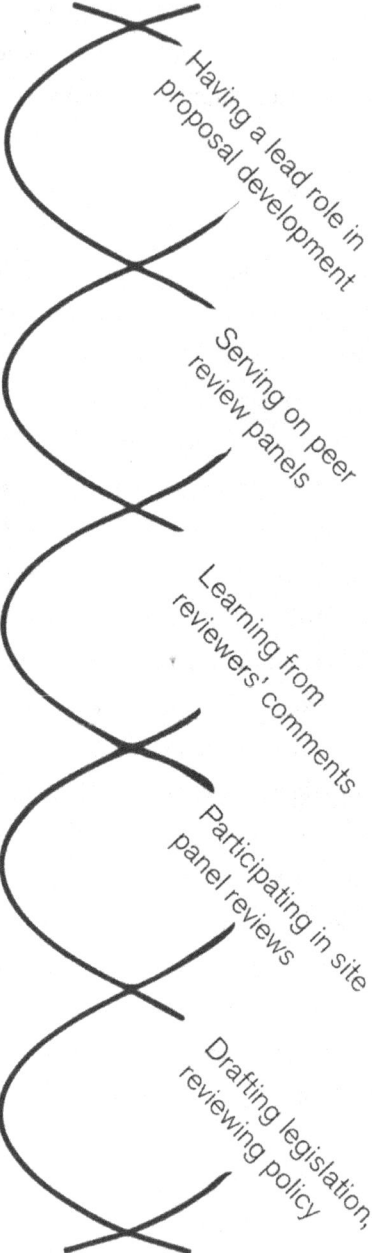

Having a lead role in proposal development

Serving on peer review panels

Learning from reviewers' comments

Participating in site panel reviews

Drafting legislation, reviewing policy

S.M.P., 2014

There are some crucial errors in the grant writing process, which we advise that you avoid. Some common ones are described following. First and foremost, as we have noted earlier, a primary reason given by review panels for not recommending a proposal for funding commonly relates to concerns about the qualifications of the applicant. This judgment also extends to the capacity of the applicant organization to host and manage the funded project effectively. For those of you on an academic path, you should do all in your power to buttress your credentials and to develop the kinds of documentable skills and experiences that would facilitate your ability to implement the funded grant with integrity. If this strategy is insufficient, then adding a senior, experienced co-principal investigator may be an acceptable alternative. For those consulting to or in professional placements within applicant organizations, your ability to network and collaborate to demonstrate mastery of the topic and proposed work could help determine the ultimate success of your grant-writing efforts. A primary reason for private funding sources not to fund a proposal stems from a gap or lack of fit between the applicant organization's values and mission and those of the funding source.

On a related matter, a common mistake that developers of otherwise fundable proposals make is that insufficient time or FTE[4] is allocated for the principal investigator(s) and project director to provide confidence that the grant activities can actually be supervised and carried out as described in the application. Notably, proposal developers (even experienced ones) often do not devote sufficient attention to relatively small point categories in the RFP (e.g. budget and cost effectiveness or dissemination plans) that are nevertheless very important to providing reviewer panel assurance that the proposed work is a sound investment of public/private funds. Further, the decision to fund or not fund a grant application is sometimes based on differences of a few points or even tenths of a point —thus, every point counts! Many grant applications are not funded due to these costly but relatively simple, avoidable mistakes and oversights.

Grant applications are not funded due to relatively simple, avoidable mistakes and oversights

Use tables and figures to graphically organize and summarize large bodies of literature

Constantly search for opportunities to summarize

---

[4] FTE = Full Time Equivalent

Using Visuals

Graphic organizers of content will greatly assist you in summarizing and integrating large bodies of information, especially when a page limit is a requirement of the proposal submission process. We have used such figures (i.e., graphic organizers) in multiple, successful grant applications.

This approach is shared here to illustrate several important points about presenting information regarding complex topics in grant applications on which considerable research has been conducted. The basic rule is *when you can use tables or figures to graphically organize and summarize large bodies of professional literature on a specific topic* it is in your great interest to do so. This strategy allows you to present important elements of an entire literature at a glance for the reader's convenience. It obviously saves enormous amounts of textual material and spares the reader the time and effort of going through it.

Using graphic organizers is a highly recommended strategy within the front end of a proposal application (e.g., making the argument for the central idea) and also in the analysis and synthesis of the evidence section(s) of the proposal. When reviewing literature associated with the topic or focus of your proposal, we recommend that you constantly search for opportunities to summarize and integrate large bodies of empirically derived information as well as commentaries and expert opinion where appropriate. As a general rule, you will need some sort of template or organizing rubric to do this. It is important that you do not use specific studies as the content of such figures but rather the key elements, features or outcomes toward which you want to direct the reviewer's attention. This process involves the use of inductive forms of logic in which you are searching for and attempting to synthesize common trends or patterns that can be identified across diverse studies or types of activity. It can be a highly effective technique when it works. It is greatly appreciated by reviewers. We cover this topic within the next chapter in detail.

Schemata[5] can also be used to frame and provide an organizing vehicle for an entire grant application as well as to a) illustrate a basic approach or model for addressing the central focus of the grant, and b) build a convincing argument for what it is you plan to do. A schema is an illustrated plan for achieving a major goal or outcome that can be diagrammatically presented. Often, a schema functions as a larger construct. This construct explains a series of related events and provides a conceptual umbrella for

---

[5] Schemata (plural); Schema (singular)

dealing with them. An example of a generic schema that has been widely used to structure entire grant applications is the organizing framework of: *Inputs, Outputs, Results,* and *Impact* (see Figure 6). This simple, four-element categorization allows you to address and integrate all the critical steps involved in the basic process for developing a proposal. In addition, it can be used to document the likely impact on the field (e.g., improved policy or practice) of a successful execution of the proposed grant.

Figure 6. Example of schema

Inputs	Outputs	Results	Impact

H.M.W., 2014

As a rule, schemata form the core of the case argument for a given grant, such as the development of a potential solution for a persisting, unsolved problem in the field. Their use is highly recommended in the grant-writing process, but they require careful scholarship, reflection, and a vision that forecasts details of their role in solving a high priority problem or addressing an urgent need. To the extent that you can master their use, your odds of success as a grant writer will improve. Schemata are extremely important in grant writing as they illustrate basic approaches to achieving the goals and objectives of a grant, as well as elements of the case-argument process. Further, as an organizing framework they offer a vehicle for integrating and coordinating all the diverse elements of a proposal.

We believe that the value of a schematic representation (i.e., a graphic presentation of information) is that it provides a visual of your approach or vision for what you are proposing and allows the reviewer to grasp it at a glance. It gives the reader a mental picture of the content addressed. Their use is highly recommended in grant writing (and in professional writing generally). Some federal agencies will provide templates to visually display information in the proposal (e.g., logic maps).

An effective schema needs to be customized and contextualized for each grant proposal. With experience you will find that, the more proposals you submit, the more ideas you will generate for creating and displaying schemata in your proposals (see Figure 6).

Once you have developed and explicated a schema that represents your approach to addressing the central argument or key goal of your application, there are steps that you must follow. These include:

a) making a convincing case for what you plan to do
b) developing a strategy or set of strategies for investigating the topic
c) presenting a coherent set of goals and objectives that are measureable and attainable
d) preparing your method, data analysis and evaluation sections
e) showing how your research (and/or practice) will advance the field, stimulate additional research, and influence policy and practices (see Figure 7).

We recommend that you study multiple examples of funded applications to see how successful investigators have approached these tasks.

Figure 7. Steps in developing a proposal

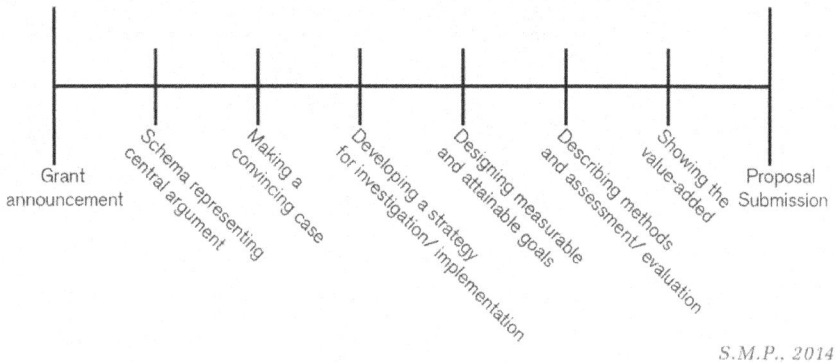

Grant announcement — Schema representing central argument — Making a convincing case — Developing a strategy for investigation/implementation — Designing measurable and attainable goals — Describing methods and assessment/evaluation — Showing the value-added — Proposal Submission

S.M.P., 2014

Developing pro and con arguments regarding potential grant foci or topical ideas can be a very useful exercise. You will need to learn when is appropriate to do so. Professional opinion is often divided on controversial policy issues, especially when the empirical evidence is not clear. It will be your important task to provide grant reviewers with a clear mental picture of the issues at hand, particularly when such issues are controversial.

Effective Use of Language

The language usage and writing skills necessary for achieving success in grant writing are highly specialized, yet scholars, researchers, and professionals in many fields can master them. A successful grant writer must have proficiency with language and an understanding of the role of logic in making persuasive, compelling arguments (see Figure 8). In this section we profile some of the attributes that many successful writers possess—as reflected, for example, in the language usage and writings of Abraham Lincoln, one of Hill's favorite writers. While you do not have to be a great writer such as Lincoln to have a successful career in grant writing, it is important for you to have a sense of what characterizes these individuals, how they used language instrumentally to achieve important outcomes, and the influence they had through this form of communication. Some modern masters of the nonfiction writing craft are David Herbert Donald, David McCullough, Doris Kearns-Goodwin, and Shelby Foote —all historians. Each has a clear, smooth, and readable writing style that is underpinned by the best scholarship —which is the standard we should all strive to meet in our professional writing. See recommended readings in Appendix A.

Figure 8. Mastery of grant writing

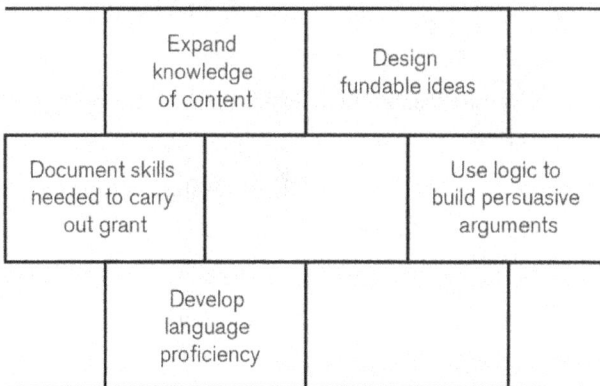

	Expand knowledge of content	Design fundable ideas	
Document skills needed to carry out grant		Use logic to build persuasive arguments	
	Develop language proficiency		

S.M.P., 2014

We find the following to be the key rules, conventions, and specific skills of critical importance in becoming an effective grant writer. These features are essential to persuasive and argumentative forms of discourse that are required in making an effective case for your proposal, as well as in constructing straightforward narratives designed to educate and share information in a more generic sense.

It is important to distinguish here between the differing types or purposes of language use. In grant writing, skilled *expository* and *argumentative* forms of writing are both important. Expository writing is characterized as discourse that is used to explain something, to share a viewpoint, and/or to provide information that clarifies an issue or problem. It is essentially descriptive in nature and involves a straightforward flow of narrative designed to convey information. *Argumentative* writing, in contrast, is designed to persuade or be enterprising with the purpose of guiding individuals' attitudes or beliefs in a certain direction. It is an instrumental use of language to achieve certain goals important to the writer. Argumentative writing is much more closely aligned with strategic story telling than is expository writing. It consists of a series of claims or premises that lead to a particular conclusion and typically relies upon the use of deductive logic, but uses inductive logic in some cases. The argumentative form of writing requires considerable skill to do well and rests upon an understanding of critical thinking and principles of logical expression.

Nationally syndicated columnists are superb masters at using these forms of discourse to influence their readers. For example, George Will is an exceptional writer in this genre, a master of metaphor and analogy, and arguably has the best command of language skills among national columnists. For centuries, lawyers have used the argumentative process to build a case for either their client's innocence or for the guilt of the accused. Lincoln, for example, was a true master of both expository and argumentative writing and used them to great effect in his legal practice, in his political life, and in his presidency. Lincoln had a technician's mastery of the structural aspects of language and a poet's imagination in the skillful use of metaphor, symbols, and images. He was able to blend these attributes into numerous, compelling examples of writing that were both inspiring and politically advantageous in defusing the arguments his political enemies directed against him. He was the ultimate master of persuasive, argumentative writing and used his legal talent and skills to great advantage in his political life.

So the question arises: what should you strive for in your writing? We propose a trifold approach: *frugality*, clarity, and *precision*. These three factors, when combined

Strive for frugality, clarity, and precision in your writing

within the context of grant writing, will allow you to communicate effectively (see Figure 9). If you develop a broad and diverse vocabulary, become familiar with the rules and structural features of correct language usage, and understand thoroughly the use of logic in making a case, you will have mastered the foundational elements of good professional writing and communication. Mastery of your subject matter (i.e., your topic of focus) is equally important, as is intimate knowledge of the key terms and concepts in your professional specialization(s).

As we have emphasized, it is important to remember that professional writing is largely an acquired skill and there are conventions associated with it that enhance its effectiveness if followed carefully. This is particularly important when pursuing private funding because you need to assume that your readers will not have mastery over the content. How you express your proposal in writing can define your ability to secure funding.

Figure 9. Effective written communication

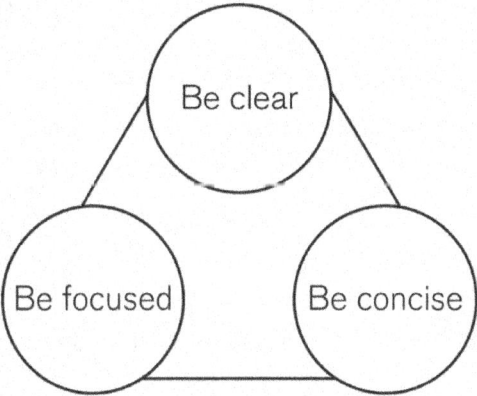

H.M.W. & S.M.P., 2014

Lincoln was a writer who regarded language as the greatest invention of human kind. He said it allowed long dead writers to communicate with those living in the present and it enabled present and future generations of writers to communicate with those who come after them. Language is indeed a remarkable instrument and enables the transmission of essential knowledge across generations, epochs, and even millennia. Scholars increasingly regard Lincoln as the greatest president of this country. This assessment is due in no small part to the fact that, in addition to being one of the greatest political leaders this country has ever seen, he was also an unquestioned literary genius. Through his remarkably skilled use of language and the vivid emotional images and metaphors that he was able to craft, Lincoln galvanized public opinion at key points in the Civil War to sustain the nation's support for the Union cause.

Perhaps the most interesting feature of Lincoln's use of language is how simple and uncomplicated his writing appears. He did not use any words that were not in common usage at the time. Yet it was his arrangement of the words and the iconic, symbolic meaning(s) of his phrases that so captured his audiences. In his first inaugural address, Lincoln was desperate to persuade his fellow citizens not to go down the path of war. Following is the final sentence of his first inaugural address regarding his plea for avoiding disunion and the scourge of war.

We regard this sentence as one of the most powerful expressions we have ever seen crafted by any writer in any genre: "The mystic chords of memory, stretching from every battlefield, and patriot grave, to every living heart and hearthstone, all over this broad land, will yet swell the chorus of the Union, when again touched, as surely they will be, by the better angels of our nature".

This example offers a perspective for grant writers about how to identify great writing. While Lincoln's words represent syntax pertinent to the nineteenth century, they are indeed simple. As noted, it is the arrangement of his words that makes the passages so elegant and powerful. When Lincoln's prose is subjected to a language analysis using current computer software programs, where it is analyzed along different dimensions, the results tend to reveal simple, uncomplicated writing. Aside from his simple but elegant use of language, there are other valuable lessons for us in Lincoln's writing. For example, he had a tremendous mastery of the basic structure of language and was a devoted student of grammar. Lincoln was a frequent user of metaphor and analogy, which added great power to his writing. He had a vast vocabulary and was widely read in history, philosophy and, literature.

Language allows long dead writers to communicate with those living in the present and enables present and future generations of writers to communicate with those who come after them
– Lincoln

The writer has responsibility for not only what is said but also for what is read, taken away, and remembered
– Luntz

It is extremely important that your proposal be perceived as interesting, new or innovative, and well put together

Lincoln's general approach to using language can serve to inform grant writers in this century about how to design and arrange passages in proposals in a way that allows them to become persuasive storytellers through the process of securing funding.

We are convinced that the more knowledgeable you are about the rules and conventions of language and the more widely read you are in your field and areas related to it, the more advantaged you will generally be in the grant-writing process. We believe these things will also make the writing process easier and less burdensome. We propose that the writer has responsibility for not only what is said but also for what is read, taken away, and remembered (Luntz, 2007). Luntz developed ten rules of successful communication. These are:

1) Ask questions
2) Offer something new
3) Provide context and explain relevance
4) Use simple language (e.g., use small words)
5) Be brief (e.g., use short sentences)
6) Be consistent
7) Visualize
8) Speak aspirationally
9) Credibility is as important as philosophy
10) Sounds and texture matter

Although these rules of effective communication and use of language were not developed with grant writing in mind, they have considerable relevance to this more technical form of writing. In grant writing you are communicating with a set of reviewers who, at the outset, are not inclined to fund your proposal.

In fact, some reviewers may opt to support funding your grant *only* if they cannot find a defensible reason not to do so. Such reviewers are a very difficult sell. Skilled language use, along with a powerful proposal idea, is likely one of your very best means for persuading them. So to connect with reviewers like these, who populate many review panels it is extremely important that your proposal be perceived as interesting, new or innovative, and well put together.

In this context, language correctness assumes great importance. When submitting a proposal for review in a grant competition, there can be NO grammatical errors. If your application is riddled with incorrect language usage and/or spelling errors, you project carelessness and lack of attention to detail to your reviewers. This characterization

Carefully proof and edit your application

may not be true of you in a general sense. However, the reviewer is in no position to know that! Once you have prepared your grant as well as you can, it is essential that you proof it carefully so that all errors, glitches, and anomalies are identified and corrected. If you are unsure of yourself in this regard, then it is best to access a copyeditor with the skills to carefully proof and edit your application. Many professionals have had to absorb this lesson through painful, direct experience. In our experience, having a second reader review the proposal before it has been submitted has proven instrumental in helping to secure much of our success with grants.

Finally, we believe it is sometimes the case that what is most important to the author of a grant proposal is not perceived as such by reviewers. The sheer number of applications they have to review and report on within panel deliberations often overwhelms reviewers. Because grant applicants are frequently overly cautious about being accused of redundancy, they sometimes err in the other direction and do not sufficiently emphasize the case being made or the seminal points that the reader needs to hear and take away. That said, overly redundant writing does carry some risk of irritating the reviewer. There is a technique that some sophisticated grants persons use to address this challenge called *creative redundancy* (see Figure 10). That is, you say the same thing in different ways, multiple times throughout the proposal. If this technique is used appropriately, you can subtly reinforce your key points in the proposal without inducing cognitive dissonance in the reviewer. However, like excessive redundancy, creative redundancy does carry some obvious risks and it should be used with discretion. The advantage associated with it is that the reviewer is more likely to hear and remember what you say as a result of its use. A good example of creative redundancy is the last chapter in this book, which reviews the important points presented within the previous chapters and provides some key takeaway lessons.

Figure 10. Creative redundancy

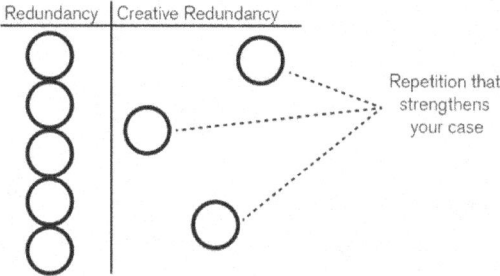

S.M.P., 2014

Strategies and Approaches for Learning the Grant Writing Process

This section briefly describes information sources and activities that can enhance your skill development regarding the grant writing process. These include: 1) resources, 2) study, 3) service, 4) volunteer opportunities, 5) programs, and 6) partnerships.

1. **Resources** – Generic references and resources on successful grant writing provide boundaries to your knowledge base, helping you to develop a clear understanding of your skill set and capacity as a grant writer. These constructs will serve you well when designing and producing grant proposals, and when marketing your grant writing skills to clients. Some of these generic resources may include:

- Books
- Instructional manuals
- Tip sheets
- Resources published by the Grants Center[6]
- Commercially sponsored grant writing workshops
- University coursework in grant writing and project management

2. **Study** – Applying yourself to studying successful grant applications that have been funded can potentially help you to identify trends and patterns of successful grant writing, as well as criteria for decision-making from reviewers. Possible avenues for accessing these include:

- Federal and State agencies that procure and make awards via
- competitive grants
- Review panels convened by funding organizations
- (e.g., foundation Board members and staff)
- Development directors and/or grant writers who capture
- feedback on each proposal

3. **Service** – Serving on as many review panels as possible will be invaluable in your understanding of the funding process. It will also inform your grant-writing choices. The experience will allow you to directly observe the evaluation process used to determine a proposal's fundability. Some ways in which you can access this experience include:

- Ask to be placed on a list of peer reviewers – volunteer your

---

[6] http://www.apts.org/grantcenter

time and expertise with national organizations in your field
of interest

- Become a Rotarian – learn from their international and local
community-based proposal system by serving on their review
committees

4. **Volunteer Opportunities** – Affiliate and volunteer your time and effort with professionals who have successfully negotiated the grant procurement process. Networking with grant writers will give you access to first-hand knowledge and experience about the demands and rewards of grant writing. Opportunities for volunteering include:

- Local nonprofits – shadow/work with grant writers,
Development/Executive Directors, Board members
- Public institutions – identify professional grant writers
in school districts, cities, counties, and hospitals
- Higher education institutions – most all these institutions
have foundation and development officers responsible for
grant writing; if possible, build a network of these individuals
in your community

5. **Programs** – Businesses and larger corporations (especially if you are in a big city) are likely to have a foundation or corporate responsibility office. Learn about their efforts for giving to the community. Look for new-investigator grant opportunities and/or student initiated grant programs. While these opportunities are specific to those of you interested in furthering your academic careers, the same concept applies to early-career professionals who are interested in building a portfolio of awarded proposals. Possible ways in which you can do this include:

- Micro-awards funded by financial institutions in your
community (e.g., banks)
- Internal funding opportunities channeled by national
chapters or organizations (e.g., Boys and Girls Club of America)

6. **Partnerships** – Consider fellowships or internships with investigator groups that are well known and respected in the field. If in academia, identify researchers who have a demonstrated record of successful grant writing in your field of inquiry and expertise. If located professionally in your community, identify organizations that have successfully secured funding to mobilize mission-based efforts via grant writing. Examples may include:

- Higher education institutions – University of Kansas (Juniper Gardens); University of Oregon (Center for Teaching and Learning; Educational & Community Supports); Indiana University (Center on Philanthropy – IUPUI)
- Research institutions – Oregon Social Learning Center (OSLC); Oregon Research Institute (ORI); The Getty Research Institute (GRI); The Stanford Research Institute (SRI)

Story Telling through Numbers

Your ability to storytell through numbers can be as important as the quality of the content in the proposal

You should always try to work closely with a business manager or fiscal officer when developing a budget for a grant proposal

Along with the category of personnel, determining the budget and potential cost effectiveness of an award (i.e., funded proposal) is one of the most important information areas for reviewers and funding sources alike. As a rule, the budget and cost effectiveness category within a grant proposal is assigned up to 15% of the total points allocated to an application. However, it is a very important share of the available points, and its overall influence often outweighs its actual point value. This is because your ability to story-tell through numbers (i.e., give a mental picture) can be as important as the quality of the content in the proposal.

Typically, the budget categories within a research or model development application are as follows: personnel, fringe benefits, travel, equipment, supplies, printing and reproduction, and other. You will also have to calculate an overhead or indirect rate, which is the share or percentage of the total budget that the submitting agency (e.g., university, research institution) has previously negotiated with the federal government. Overhead rates for grants can range from 8% to well over 50% of total budget categories depending upon the type of grant being submitted. Typically, research grants require a much higher overhead rate than model demonstration, training, or outreach grants. Your budget, with costs summed across all budget categories plus the indirect or overhead rate figure added to this amount, represents the total cost of the proposal. Standard printed forms are usually included in the budget pages section of the RFP that is used to create and post the budget. This section will also contain detailed instructions for constructing and justifying the budget (see Appendix C).

For local or private funding proposals, the budget section is customized to the funding source's capacity or the specific RFP as posted. For example, for most posted opportunities, the total award requested is expected to be applied to direct services or programs versus operational or administrative costs. Hence, the format for displaying the budget in these proposals is usually not provided by the funding source and needs to be customized depending on the specific award being pursued. For flow-through awards from state or federal funds (e.g., a national nonprofit receives federal funding and encourages internal competition by local affiliates across the country), the same expectations as described in the paragraph above apply.

The budget categories in a grant proposal are used, as a rule, to calculate detailed costs for the first year of the award (for local or private funding, these are typically used to calculate total award costs). Budget estimates for the award's remaining years are usually required, yet not in the level of detail as for the first year. Often, an inflationary increase not exceeding 5% per year is allowed by the funding agency. However, this can vary substantially across agencies (this increase, in general, does not apply to local or private funding opportunities). Some general guidelines for developing a budget for your application are listed below:

Never submit a budget that exceeds the total cost of the grant application as posted in the RFP

1. You should always try to work closely with a business manager or fiscal officer when developing a budget for a grant proposal. If you are affiliated with a small business or nonprofit, you may be able to access sufficient information (organization-wide) to produce a proposed budget for approval (by the CEO and/or Board of Directors). Nevertheless, it is our recommendation that you seek advice from professionals to review and revise your work as needed whenever possible. For proposals submitted through higher education institutions, it is best to involve this person early on in the budgetary process as they likely possess information about the submitting agency and federal rules of which you may not be aware. Other benefits may include time savings, efficient efforts, and accuracy of compliance with budgetary rules.

2. The budget instructions included in the RFP should be followed to the letter. If an issue is unclear, you should contact the funding agency/source for clarification rather than risk making a costly mistake or misinterpretation of a budget requirement. For local and private funding, in particular during a national economic crisis or downturn, clarity and accuracy in the budget section could heavily influence your funding chances.

3. As a rule, the RFP will include an upper limit for the total cost of the grant application that is allowable. *Never submit a budget that exceeds this amount.* In general, develop budgets that target average awards published by the funding source. If your project needs a higher funding budget, make sure to have ongoing and clear conversations with the funding agency's manager or fund administrator to monitor a) the progress of your proposal and b) their continued interest in funding it at the necessary level for the success of your project. Private and local funding sources are more likely to fund "as necessary" depending on the project.

4. It is a good idea to examine a series of budgets from previously funded grants to get a sense of how they are constructed. This is considered a best practice because it will provide you with "common language" and a structure expected by reviewers and funders.

Key personnel in a proposal must be qualified for the roles they are expected to carry out

5. When preparing your budget justification (narrative), it is very important to show how every single budget category amount is essential or reasonable and that its cost is defensible/ necessary. This is extremely important for the fund administrators or agency/program managers who are assigned to the grant proposal/project in order to carry out its planned activities. Excessive salaries that surpass expected normative levels are an indication of potential misallocations in a proposal's budget. For private and local funding, make sure to research average salary trends (both nationally and in your area) to meet these expectations.

6. You must think very carefully about the amount of FTE[7] that is assigned to key personnel in the proposed project/award. As a rule, it is risky to assign less than 0.20FTE to a project director who is primarily responsible for project leadership and/or implementation. This person usually manages personnel, oversees implementation, and secures compliance with award requirements (e.g., reporting). Many grant proposals are rejected because the funder and/or the panel of reviewers do not believe the work can be accomplished with the assigned FTE. You can have two or even three co-principal investigators (Co-PIs) on a proposal, but their respective roles and project activities must be carefully justified and their FTE amounts well documented. Co-PIs' FTE allocations generally range from 0.05FTE to 0.15FTE. Unless there is a compelling reason for it, a proposal should not be submitted in which two individuals share equally in its management and FTE amounts. This is important so that reviewers and funders are able to identify one individual who is ultimately responsible for achieving project goals and objectives. All these general rules apply to private and local funding as well, yet the scope of leadership varies, usually identifying one manager or administrator and direct service providers (for program/project implementation).

7. It is important to highlight that key personnel in a proposal must be qualified for the roles they are expected to carry out, that their assigned FTE is adequate to the tasks they must perform, and that they are reasonably compensated given their level of training and expertise. When creating positions within a budget for personnel who are judged essential for ensuring the project's success, it is indispensable that each position is actually required for the proposed project's success. Bolstering a personnel budget in a proposal for the purpose of maintaining/extending agency FTEs should never happen unless these individuals are vital to the successful implementation of the project.

8. Some applications require an in-kind or local contribution (i.e., cost share) by the submitting organization, which is a form of jointly sharing certain costs of the project. This in-kind contribution often takes the form of FTE from the submitting organization, which is paid for by other fiscal sources. These

---

[7] FTE – Full Time Equivalent as it refers to employment (i.e., time effort).

9. funds are used to achieve proposal objectives and/or to support project operations. For example, operational costs like accounting services or leasing physical space, as well as the assigned FTE of an expert related to the proposal —statistics, design, measurement, evaluation. These costs can add up to 25% of the total budget and they sometimes prevent a potential applicant from submitting a proposal if the in-kind contribution cannot be met. This issue must be negotiated with the submitting organization's leader. This person should be brought into the decision process as soon as possible. In the case of small businesses or nonprofits, this negotiation might refer to more than one individual, like the Board of Directors. A related issue has to do with the use of real versus potential numbers when reporting the in-kind contribution. The calculated in-kind contribution should easily be able to pass an independent audit as to its appropriateness and accuracy. This expectation applies to submitting organizations in both academia and industry. Local and private funders, in general, do not expect an in-kind contribution as part of the grant proposal.

10. The budget is your best estimate of the funds necessary to cover the salaries and benefits of staff at the time of the grant's submission. The amounts budgeted and those actually paid in salary may differ and are subject to a number of influencing factors (e.g., total amount awarded; changes in economic trends, like cost of living adjustments), which make it less than a perfect relationship or one-to-one correspondence. Hence, we recommend that negotiations with staff over salaries occur before the budget is finalized and submitted as a part of the grant proposal. If you have never done this before, partner with an experienced grant writer, development director, financial manager, researcher, and/or decision maker who can guide you through a) the process of assessing the impact of these decisions on stakeholders' lives and b) the importance of timing and transparent communication about these decisions.

11. If the funder does not allow for annual cost of living adjustments (i.e., COLA) as part of the potential award, then you may have to underspend in some of the budget categories in order to compensate for this limitation. As a rule, federal awards may allow up to a 5% divergence between budget category amounts and actual expenditures —provided the total budget is not overspent. For local and

private awards, COLA expenditures may be categorized as administrative or operational costs, and therefore not allowed.

To reiterate, the budgetary cost effectiveness of your proposal must be clearly demonstrated in order for it to be funded. This is often a jointly derived decision by panel reviewers, funding agency project officers, and fund managers. All areas of a grant proposal are important but none is more important than the budget. Remember that you should strive to get every single point available in this section of the application and that each and every budget category is important in this regard. The budget section of the grant proposal is a good example of how grant writing is an art. Your job in this section is to story-tell through numbers.

This chapter attempts to provide you with a sense of the grant writing landscape and identify some of the critical skills (e.g., proficient language usage, applications of principles of logic) that are, in our view, required elements of successful grant writing. We have also imparted some "nuts and bolts" of wisdom about this process from lessons we have learned over the years as grant writers. Such knowledge is difficult to come by and is most often acquired through direct experience. The following chapter provides you with some essential knowledge about the foundations of the grant writing and proposal development process.

Chapter III
The Foundations of Successful Grant Writing

In this chapter, we purposefully designed the sections that we have identified as core to successful grant writing in bullet list format to facilitate your ability to grasp and remember these concepts. We begin the chapter by making explicit the profile of a successful grant writer, followed by an overview of the grant writing process. We categorized this overview in four sections to help you develop a systemic understanding of the process. We conclude the bulleted format of content with a review of the social component in grant writing and the development of competitive applications. The following sections in this chapter use a descriptive approach to catalogue ways of developing compelling arguments, using critical thinking strategies, making an effective case, and building case arguments.

Profile of a Grant Writer

Together, we have more than four decades of experience in grant writing, both as lead grant writers and as members of teams submitting competitive proposals for funding. In our experience, there are core components to the performance of a successful grant writer that define his/her success in the field. In an effort to make explicit our embedded knowledge, we describe these components here to provide you with the profile of a successful grant writer (see Figure 11). We have touched on some of the attributes comprising this profile earlier herein, but treat them in detail in the following narrative. The titles to each section below are identified by one word to help you remember the content. These components are:

Grant writing is very much like a competitive sport

Negotiate with your family and friends the responsibilities associated with grant writing

- **Identity** – *You must have a competitive nature.* Having a competitive nature and enjoying, at some level, taking risks and putting yourself on the line to be judged by others will be helpful in your application process. Grant writing is very much like a competitive sport. You will need to find a way to stand out from the hundreds of grant proposals

- **Value** – *You have to negotiate with your family and friends about the value of grant writing.* You have to be willing to give up some vacations, evenings, and some weekends as necessary to produce a quality grant application that will be judged against a pool of possibly hundreds of other applications where only ten to fifteen percent will be funded. If you can successfully negotiate with your family and friends the responsibilities associated with grant writing (e.g., timing for submittal, attention to detail), you can increase your chances for a prosperous and long-lasting career as a grant writer.

Ability in using language fluently, persuasively, and creatively is a must

Attention to detailed expectations from the funder will increase your chances to secure an awarded proposal

Learning to collaborate intelligently could help you to stand out in a competitive funding setting

- **Vision** – *Give boundaries to your vision for each grant proposal.* Give boundaries to your vision for each grant proposal and understand that on occasion possibly the only thing worse than not being funded is actually being funded. Most people focus on addressing errors made or goals not achieved, yet few address the impact of doing a good job. If you understand the responsibilities attached to successfully securing funding through your grant writing, you will be better positioned to manage yours and your client's expectations about next steps (e.g., reporting, budgeting, implementation, assessment, fundraising for scalability).

- **Capacity** – *Ability in using language fluently, persuasively, and creatively is a must.* This ability is a requirement and you will need to continue developing these skills throughout your grant-writing career. Discover ways in which you can find pleasure while expanding your skill set. For example, you might like watching movies. In doing so, as an exercise, pay close attention to dialogue and language structure and see how screenplay writing differs from your grant writing style. Could this writing style be incorporated into your grant writing process? Do similar exercises when reading or chatting with others.

- **Skills** – Careful and consistent attention to detailed expectations from the funder will increase your chances of securing a funded proposal. Careful and consistent attention to minute details, bordering on being obsessive-compulsive, is a characteristic of most successful grant writers. As you gain experience in grant writing, you will find that most funders are very specific about their expectations during the submission process. Some funders focus on length (e.g., no more than 20 pages), other focus on structure (e.g., size of margins, style of font, space between lines, number of lines per page), others focus on content (e.g., specific order for sections of content), and yet others focus on everything! It will be your job as a grant writer to make sure that all grantor expectations are met as you draft the grant proposal for submission. Paying attention to these detailed expectations from the funder will increase your chances to secure an awarded proposal.

- **Strategy** – *Learning to collaborate intelligently could help you to stand out in a competitive funding setting.* Networking and collaboration are trademarks of the skill set you must develop in order to secure prominent funding opportunities. At the onset of the book, we offered a brief overview of funding trends early in the 21st century. The likelihood of needing to develop and submit collaborative proposals to secure funding continues to increase due to strained economic environments across the country. Hence, a better understanding of your professional and personal identity, and learning to collaborate intelligently could help you to stand out in a competitive funding setting.

- **Resilience** – *You are likely to improve your performance as a grant writer the longer you continue to write grants.* Persistence and resiliency in the face of failure are essential requirements. Learning how to cope with and manage your own expectations (i.e., psychological, cognitive, professional) and those of your client (e.g., management practices, timing for project/program/research implementation, congruence with funder's mission) will become essential to your ability to navigate the grant-writing experience successfully over a prolonged period. There is a high likelihood that in the process of refining your grant-writing skills, reviewers may misunderstand the core of your message. If such is the case, do not despair as you are likely to improve your performance as a grant writer the longer you continue to prepare and submit grants.

Figure 11. Profile of a grant writer

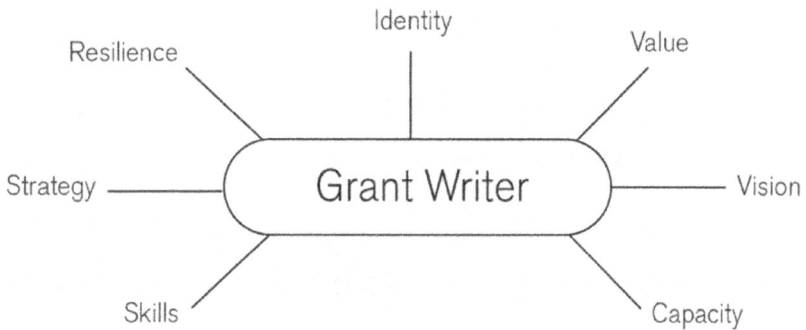

S.M.P., 2014

Grant Writing: An Overview

In this section, we have summarized in the form of bullets some key principles and strategies that you will find discussed throughout this book. We have identified four topical areas derived from our own grant-writing experiences, and that of others. We have analyzed and described them in a way that we hope can be helpful to you. These areas are: a) general concepts, b) proposals, c) reviewers, and d) logistics. Some of these principles are specific to academic environments and/or federally funded opportunities, yet most are applicable to privately funded processes as well. You will notice that the information below includes these symbols: (I) and (E). These will be represented in Figure 12 and mean I = intrinsic and E = extrinsic. These categories refer to whether you are in control of the principle identified (I) or whether the principle is impacted by systems beyond your influence (E). To the extent possible, a successful grant writer must master both intrinsic and extrinsic influences in the grant-writing ecosystem (see Figure 12).

General Concepts

- As we have noted, grant making has been in practice since the ancient pharaohs of Egypt. In spite of what you might hear about the demise of grant-application opportunities, grant making will continue to be a viable option for the government and foundations to use in addressing society's problems and achieving progress. (E)

- The grant-writing process involves the skillful use of both deductive and inductive forms of logic —you need to study and master them both. (I)

  The grant-writing process involves the skillful use of both deductive and inductive forms of logic

- The grant-writing process could be considered analogous to a situation in which you are a beginning attorney and your task is to persuade a jury, stacked against you, about the merits of your client's position in a case involving steep odds against success. (E)

- The case-argument process used so effectively by attorneys and nationally syndicated columnists has enormous relevance to constructing a successful grant application. If you know lawyers, talk to them in detail about the strategies they use in this process. Read the national columnists and study how they make a case for a position and support it —George Will, Maureen Dowd, Thomas Friedman, Michael Gerson, and Paul Krugman are examples of journalists who have mastered this craft exceptionally well. (E)

- One of the best sources for reading about how to write effective grant proposals includes the works of Rudolf Flesch (see Appendix A). He notes that one of the great tragedies of academia is all the books and scholarly pieces that professors have in them that never get out and see the light of day due to a lack of discipline and motivation or competing priorities. (I)

- Remember that no matter how successful you have been as a grant writer, you are only as good as your last grant —you do not know when you might get awarded another one. (I)

- Importantly, everyone has a slightly different spin on what it takes to be successful in the field of grant writing. Listen to as many points of view as possible, solicit as much advice as you can, and take it all (including the content in this book) with a grain of salt. (E)

Proposals

- There is no substitute for a brilliant or compelling idea around which to build a grant application. In general, the better the idea, the less weight the application per se has to carry. (I)

- The best ideas for grant applications involve proposing solutions to pressing, unsolved problems, or solutions that address clear gaps in the existing knowledge base. (E)

- There is the possibility that your very best ideas and proposals may not be funded —the goal is to develop and submit as many quality applications as you can in order to maximize your chances over time and across your career. (E)

- There can be no conceptual or methodological holes, flaws, or obvious weaknesses in what you propose to do. This is when networking and collaboration become core to the success of your grant proposal. Try to access experts throughout the grant-writing process to review your methods as is feasible. (E)

- The grant-writing process is now so competitive that you must walk a fine line between what is proposed and promising more than you can deliver. (I)

- Try to develop a title for your grant application that forms an acronym that carries meaning for what you propose. For example, project RETAIN for an application dealing with preventing school dropout, or project PROACT for an application focusing on early intervention to prevent antisocial behavior at the point of school entry. (I)

- Publish in the general areas in which you plan to write research grants. For those of you who are not in academia, try to affiliate your professional performance with institutions that have the capacity to carry forward the outlined work in the grant proposals. Focus on building a consistent organizational performance record across time. (I)

- Develop research proposals that will investigate potential solutions to social, educational, cultural, or economic problems of importance. Study new federal initiatives and legislation carefully. Analyze the types of needs and challenges created by them. (I)

Reviewers

- We argue herein that one of the best sources of information on how to prepare a successful application is to serve on peer review panels and observe how proposals get treated by panel members. (E)

- Connect with the funding agencies in which you are interested (in writing or in person). Actively ask a) to be a reviewer (they are always looking for them), and b) to have access to copies of recent grant applications they have funded. Study these carefully as exemplars of the standards you have to meet if you expect to be funded. These should serve as models for your grant-development efforts. (E)

- We encourage you to identify potential problems with what you are proposing and with your strategies; pre-correct rather than having the reviewer or panel as a whole do it in your stead —if you do it, you earn their respect and perhaps praise; if they do it for you, it is unlikely that your application will be funded. (I)

- The reviewers will require written proof in the proposal that you (and/or your client) have the skills, experience, institutional capacity, and knowledge necessary to carry out, with integrity, what was proposed. (E)

- Grant reviewers individually, and peer review panels collectively, look for reasons not to fund your application rather than reasons to fund it. If they cannot find any specific, defensible reasons to defund it, your proposal has a good chance to be awarded. (E)

- Read with an electron microscope the instructions and guidelines for preparing the application —follow the instructions to the letter or your grant proposal may not be reviewed. (I)

- Devote as much attention and care to the small-point categories in the application as you do to the large-point categories. It is very important to remember that, for federally funded awards, the difference between a funded and rejected grant application is often tenths or even hundredths of one point averaged across three or four reviewers. This also applies to privately funded awards. (I)

- Have colleagues review a good early version of the application using the categories, point allocations, and assessment rubric that reviewers will use once it has been submitted. You should strive to earn every point available in each category. (E)

- Grant applications that are experimental or longitudinal in nature are generally more highly regarded by review panels than other types. Also, those that are realistic and concrete are well received. (I)

- For federally funded awards, you must try to capture the attention (buy-in) of the reader in the first five to ten pages of the application and convince him or her that what you are proposing is essential to the field's progress. For private or local funding, which can involve shorter proposals, the first page might even make the difference between being considered and ending up in the recycling bin. Reviewers reject most grant proposals in the introduction or problem statement section of the proposal. While your proposal's chances of being funded may be ultimately determined by how you handle later sections of the application, if the initial case argument is not compelling and persuasive, your proposal will likely have no chance to prevail. (I)

- Consider carefully opportunities and challenges about whether you should build your application around strategies or approaches that are controversial and about which reviewers are likely to be divided (e.g., direct instruction, full inclusion, facilitated communication, behavior modification, expansion and scalability). Your proposal may not receive funding simply because individual reviewers may choose to indulge their philosophical biases and rate yours down as a result —it has happened many times in the past and will happen many times in the future. (E)

- As we have noted, most applications are rejected because panel members do not believe the project director or institution has the capacity to conduct the proposed activities successfully. If in academia and starting your career, think about affiliating with a more experienced investigator who has a successful track record. Also, respond to new-investigator competitions designed for those who are new to the field. If in industry, affiliate with an organization that already has a good track record in fundraising and/or which has a concrete mission for program/project implementation (e.g., feeding the hungry, preventing disease, addressing youth homelessness). (E)

Logistics

- As a general rule, apply for the average announced award amount of the grant. (I)

- For access to federally funded awards, subscribe to grants.gov for announcements of upcoming grant competitions. (I)

- Focus on the study of allocations of federal agencies' resources across funding and priority areas. (I)

- For access to privately funded awards, study funding cycles for industry (e.g., banks, businesses), and guidelines and RFPs posted on funders' websites (e.g., Seattle Foundation, Oregon Community Foundation). (I)

- Assess your capacity and match the content of your proposal with your funder's needs and values. When possible, promise to deliver new knowledge, empirically based outcomes, products and/or tools, and measures. This will likely increase your proposal's chance of being funded. (I)

- For federally funded awards, identify areas of the national budget that support research (i.e., field initiated research, agency directed research competitions, model development, and demonstration and special projects). (E)

- Depending on the award, the proposal, and your (your client's) capacity, consider buying (i.e., hiring out) expertise in research design, statistics, measurement, curricula and instruction, data analysis, evaluation, and/or other areas as needed. Depending on award restrictions, you may be able to include some or all of these expenses in the budget for the grant proposal. (E)

- Consider collaborating with school districts and other agencies in developing consortium grants. This will often result in a strong proposal with a good chance of funding as substantial amounts of these agencies' funding are supplied by federal flow-through dollars to states. (E)

- Develop a solid dissemination plan that is not an afterthought, but an important part of the application. (I)

The Social Component of Grant Writing

It is understood that human relationships can be quite complex within a range of settings and situations, including environments in academia and industry. The field of grant writing is no exception. There is a powerful social component embedded within the grant-writing process. This social component is sophisticated and difficult to manage effectively, but it has the potential to yield substantial advantages if you are successful at it. While you may or may not wish to engage in this part of the grant-writing process, some of your competitors will inevitably excel at managing this environment to their advantage. If you decide to play this card in the grant writing and submission process, we recommend the following strategies so that you may develop the necessary skill to compete more effectively in this context. Following are some specific strategies for you to consider in this regard:

- Study and analyze the agencies you target for grant applications. You could do this in much the same way you would research literature on a topic of interest. Agencies operate off both public (formal) and sub-rosa (informal, not published) rules. You need to be thoroughly familiar with both sets of rules, and establish networking and professional relationships with fund/program managers at these agencies. (I)

- Get to know fund/program officers in terms of how they think, their philosophical biases, their styles of operation and decision-making, and so forth. Becoming a grant reviewer is one of the very best vehicles for doing this. Through this process, you get to know the fund/program officer/s and they get to know you. (I)

- If a fund/program officer asks you to serve on a task force, participate in a site visit, or assist in developing a review of the knowledge base on a particular topic, say "yes," and accept the task. Whenever you receive requests of this type, there is one correct answer and it is always "yes," unless you have a conflict of interest. (I)

- Before an RFP is released by the funding agency, it publishes a set of priorities related to the proposed funding and asks for written comment from the field about them. Responding to this request is an excellent idea, as it allows you to shape these priorities, and thus the RFP, in your direction. Comments from the field in this context are taken very seriously by the funding agency and they provide you with an opportunity to maximize your strength(s) in the competitive process. (I)

- Beware of making political enemies in your field. If any of these individuals were to serve on review panels in grant competitions in which you are an applicant, they are in a position to fail your grant proposal as part of either the individual reviewer or panel discussion process. You always want to network with diplomacy and professionalism. (I

Figure 12. Principles of grant writing

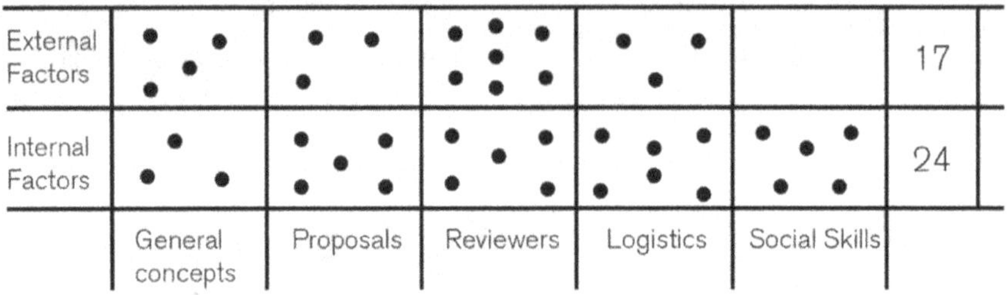

External Factors	• • •	• • •	• • • • •	• • •		17
Internal Factors	• • •	• • • •	• • • •	• • • • •	• • • • •	24
	General concepts	Proposals	Reviewers	Logistics	Social Skills	

S.M.P., 2014

Developing Competitive Applications

This process begins with fundable, compelling ideas. In this section, we identify some universal principles that you may want to consider as you practice your grant writing. These include:

- **Analysis** – Focus on analyzing new legislation to identify priorities and funding opportunities. If in academia, establish working relationships with federal and state-funded agencies to position yourself to better understand national trends and interests, as well as their fundability. If in industry, stay in close communication with local agencies (e.g., foundations, school districts), government (e.g., cities, counties), and higher education institutions (e.g., universities, community colleges) to gain common language and facilitate discourse about pressing issues. Examples to illustrate such an approach would include analyzing the Individuals With Disabilities Education Act, the No Child Left Behind Act, and the new Autism Legislation for new priorities, emerging needs, and their policy practice implications. It is important to remember that new programs of legislation such as these create many funding opportunities around requirements or demands for new instruments, interventions and decision-making procedures.

- **Approach** – Consider adoption of a problem-solutions or method-oriented approach. We described how some proposals are funded not only for the problem being addressed, but also by the innovative or creative way in which you propose to solve it. A problem-solutions approach emphasizes the identified problem and developing solutions to it as paramount. A method-oriented approach focuses on the research method or approach and the identified problem is less important.

- **Priorities** – Conduct a conceptual analysis of the existing and emerging knowledge base of high priority issues and topics. Forming learning communities of practice around these issues and topics of interest could mobilize efforts toward pressing agencies to authorize needed funding, such as addressing teacher burnout, school dropout, and at-risk children's school readiness skills.

- **Sensitivity** – Focus on developing sensitivity to new, emerging priorities in your field. If in academia, make sure to stay abreast of research developments that have relevance for the public interest. If in industry, have a clear understanding of depressed environments and potential solutions that will maintain public interest over the long term —beyond the urgent nature of the need at hand.

- **Inquiry** – Identify meaningful questions to pose to funding agencies:
    - What are the gaps and weaknesses in these existing knowledge bases?
    - Do these translate into identifiable needs? If, so, how and why?
    - Can you translate portions of these knowledge bases into effective practices for profitable by the public, other practitioners, and researchers?
    - What researchable priorities can you distill from identified gaps and weaknesses?
    - Can you develop instruments, tools and/or intervention programs that can be the focus of ongoing research and funding? Examples may include the Positive Behavior Interventions and Support (PBIS) program and the Diagnostic Indicators of Basic Emerging Literacy Skills (DIBELS).

Developing Compelling Arguments

In this section, we provide you with strategies for making a compelling, powerful case for what you are proposing in your grant application. We have included three areas of development (critical thinking strategies, approaches, and building arguments), with the last one having two key elements (the case argument, and claims and premises).

Your task is to capture the attention of the reviewer

As a general rule, this content is dealt with in the very front end of the grant under headings like *background of the problem, significance,* or *importance.* In this part of the proposal, your task is to capture the attention of the reviewer, to demonstrate how much your idea is needed, to illustrate its potential for solving a vexing, important and/or long-term problem, and to persuade the reviewer you have the vision and capacity to do so. It is very much the "make or break" section of the grant proposal. With federal funding opportunities, your proposal cannot prevail in a grant competition in

the first five to ten pages, but it can certainly lose any chance for funding it may have if you do not negotiate this section skillfully and in an interesting manner. Your skill in making your case shapes the reviewer's initial opinion about your proposal and its value.

Often reviewers are assigned 15 to 20 grants to read, review, and rate. Then they assemble as a panel and discuss their overall impressions and specific ratings of each grant. In order to be funded, you must receive consistently high ratings across all panel members. If yours is the last grant evaluated in this large stack of proposals by a particular reviewer, then your application had better be innovative, interesting, well organized, and as technically perfect as possible. It would benefit you to write it as though being read last were a likely rather than a remote possibility.

Critical Thinking Strategies for Use in Case Argument Development

The case argument process, using techniques of deductive logic combined with clear writing, is actually critical thinking applied to paper – Moore and Parker

In making your case, you rely almost exclusively upon what is called argumentative writing. This, of course, does not mean that you literally argue with the reader. Rather, you are making a claim and backing it up with reasons as to why that claim is true or should be accepted as fact. It has been said that the case argument process, using techniques of deductive logic combined with clear writing, is actually critical thinking applied to paper (Moore & Parker, 2012). Moore and Parker define argument as having two parts: a) a claim or central position (i.e., a case) regarding a specific issue, and b) a series of premises that are designed to support that claim or position (see Figure 13).

Figure 13. Making a case for funding

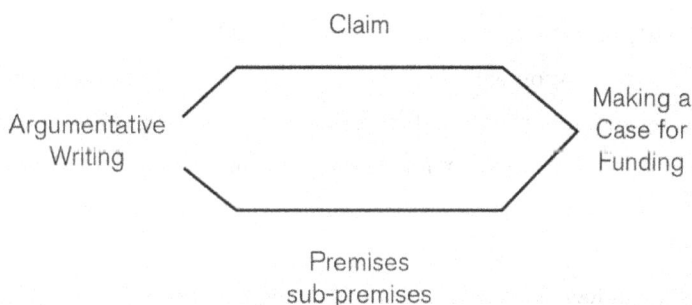

Claim

Argumentative Writing

Making a Case for Funding

Premises sub-premises

S.M.P., 2014

Premises are classified as major or minor and each can have sub-premises. Premises may take the form of such things as: assumptions, a logical analysis of trends, citing empirical evidence, documenting a critical need or priority that is widely acknowledged, or use of anecdotal information. Other examples may include prediction of dire outcomes if recommended actions are not taken, benefits to society if a new or different approach is taken, contrasting the past, present and likely future status of a societal problem (e.g., youth violence), an observation about events, and occasionally, testimony from an expert.

A diverse set of premises arranged in a logical order (e.g., from general to specific) can be very powerful in supporting a claim (see Figure 14). Premises are developed through careful research, scholarship, analysis and reflection and are then fleshed out in the case argument. Developing the premises first, and then arranging them in an order that works for you, makes writing the case argument infinitely easier! The clarity and substance of your writing will likely also be improved if you approach writing the case argument in this manner as opposed to starting from scratch or from a simple outline. We cannot overemphasize the importance of this observation strongly enough as we believe it holds true in the vast majority of cases.

Premises developed through careful research, scholarship, analysis, and reflection can support a claim when arranged in logical order

On the subject of premises, we recommend using expert testimony and commentary (e.g., in the form of quotes) only very sparingly. Reviewers will not be impressed with your ability to assemble a catalogue of expert opinion quotes within a case argument or in any other part of the grant narrative. Doing so requires very little skill and often comes across as weak. Naïve grant writers are especially prone to do this and it is considered the weakest form of documentation or support for your claim(s). However, it is most important that you carefully review, analyze, synthesize, and use professional literature and the existing knowledge base to your advantage in constructing your argument. Professional literature could include research journals, published books, and active research projects to name a few sources.

The application of logical principles and reasoning are essential to building a solid case

The application of logical principles and reasoning are essential to building a solid case. *Deductive logic*, as a rule, is most often used in the front end of a grant proposal. Inductive logic is more likely to be used in the literature review section of the grant proposal (if there is a section for one) and other parts of the proposal. Deductive logic, involving the sequential arrangement of supportive premises, is often thought of as demonstrating the validity or truth of a claim whereas inductive logic involves assembling a series of premises in support of a claim and generalizing across them to show they share certain features and are connected to the claim.

Figure 14. Arrangement of premises

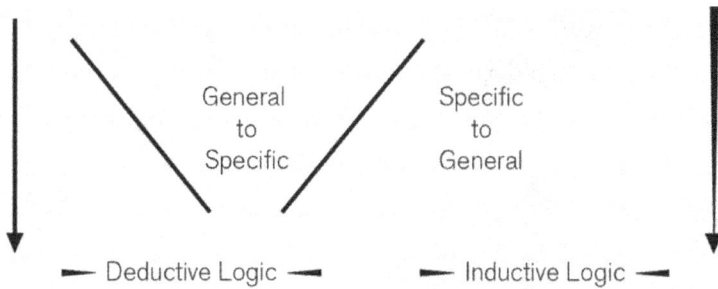

S.M.P., 2014

Deductive logic involves moving from the general to the specific, and inductive logic moves from the specific to the general. An example of inductive logic is found in direct instruction, where students are taught an instructional discrimination and then are provided with a rule that allows extrapolation to the general case. Such generalization is used to assess whether learning has occurred within this instructional paradigm. Deductive logic is similar to a geometric proof where premises follow each other and which are logically connected. A claim cannot be true or valid if the premises upon which it is based are untrue. Deductive reasoning is the thought process that allows one to demonstrate that a minor premise belongs to the class covered by a rule or principle so the one that is covered by the major premise is also covered by the minor one. That is, if A is true, then B must follow.

You judge an argument by the strength of the case made or how convincing the claim appears to be. The claim's strength, in turn, is determined by how powerful the premises are that are listed, and how persuasively they are explicated in support of the claim (Behrens, 2001). Inductive logic is known for its role in statistics and research design, where it is invoked to establish the relationship between a representative sample and a larger population to which the sample results can be generalized or applied. The more closely the sample represents the larger population, the more valid the generalization of results based upon it. The use of this logic is especially preferred by private funders. We have found inductive logic to be especially useful in analyzing and organizing knowledge bases and professional literatures to support and reinforce the central case of a proposal. If you want to develop mastery of these forms of logic and reasoning, we recommend you study the classic text by Moore and Parker (2012) on critical thinking, as we believe it sets the standard of excellence for clarity and use of logical principles in critical thinking and technical writing (see Figure 15).

Figure 15. Judging an argument

| Successful Proposal | **=** | Strength of Argument | ◀ | Making a case | ◀ | Making a claim | ◀ | Premises supporting a claim |

S.M.P., 2014

In resorting to some "creative redundancy" here, it cannot be emphasized too strongly that you think carefully about possible alternative explanations or flaws in your argument(s) within the proposal you are developing. This is especially true within the case argument section of the proposal where flaws or alternative explanations, suggested by reviewers, are most likely to occur, and be detected. Reviewers in general will respect you much more if you point out these potential weaknesses and deal with them yourself rather than having them do it for you. If the latter occurs, reviewers may assume you have not thought about them and judge your grant proposal negatively for your perceived lack of insight or sensitivity. By anticipating these flaws and offering a plan for correcting or explaining them (a process called "pre-correction") you protect yourself against this risk and possibly earn the reviewers' respect.

This phenomenon offers one of the very best reasons for having your proposal read and critiqued by trusted colleagues/peers before submission. They may bring perspectives to the review process that are quite different from yours and thus offer valuable insights or advice about the application that could be highly beneficial. This feedback will help you decide on the types of counterarguments you may need to consider developing in order to make the proposal as "airtight" as possible. In our experience as grant writers, we have seldom written grants alone, yet have often developed the initial draft and led much of the conceptualization process for them. We believe that grants written collaboratively are, for the most part, more likely to be superior to the ones written in full by one person.

Approaches to Making an Effective Case

There are four major approaches to framing a grant application and building a persuasive case for it. These are: 1) the *Question-Answer* Case Argument approach, 2) the *Review, Critique and Solve* Case Argument approach, 3) the *Theory-Action* Case Argument approach, and 4) the *Linear, Deductive* Case Argument approach (see Figure 16). We have found from our direct experiences that the last approach can be highly effective and fits well with our individual styles. However, many grant writers have used approaches 1-3 to their great advantage and, for that reason, you should know about them. In this section, we briefly review and discuss the first three approaches. The Linear, Deductive Case Argument approach will be addressed in the last section of this chapter.

Figure 16. Approaches to building a case argument (strategy)

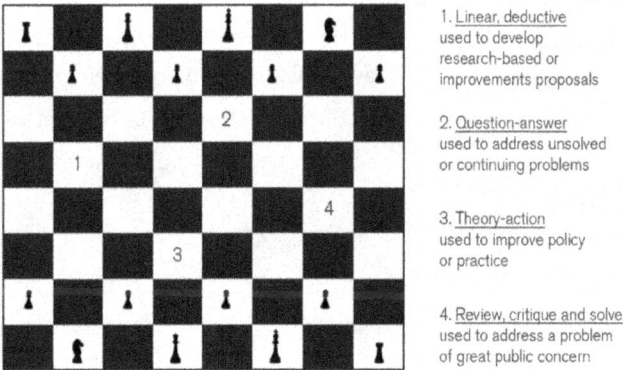

1. Linear, deductive
used to develop
research-based or
improvements proposals

2. Question-answer
used to address unsolved
or continuing problems

3. Theory-action
used to improve policy
or practice

4. Review, critique and solve
used to address a problem
of great public concern

S.M.P., 2014

Question-Answer Case Argument Approach

In this approach, a series of questions is posed relating to the past and current state of the knowledge base in the priority area or the specific problem addressed by the grant proposal. Answers are then provided through narrative explanation and graphics that allow the writer to shape the reviewers' impression(s) in the desired direction. This can be an effective strategy and is most useful when writing a proposal that seeks to develop better ways of addressing an unsolved, continuing problem that the public wants solved. Examples could include school student-dropout rates, delinquent behavior, school safety, and bullying and peer harassment, particularly cyberbullying using social media,

which has emerged as a very serious problem of public concern. These are examples of macro level social problems that have great resonance with the public, federal agency staff, and panel reviewers, and are social problems perceived as being urgently in need of better solutions. As such, these types of social problems provide excellent opportunities for grant proposals to address them.

Review, Critique, and Solve Case Argument Approach

Although this approach bears some similarity to the above described one, it begins with a general review of the topic and its historical emergence as a need or problem to be solved by some change (e.g., new legislation), a coalescing of events, or an emerging trend. Examples of such topics may include the broad consensus around the need to identify students at the beginning of their school careers who are likely to be struggling readers by the end of grade 3 or the importance of identifying and supporting adolescents who are likely to develop severe depression in high school. Other examples may include the escalating level of risk that students experience who drop out of school early, and the demands created by the No Child Left Behind Act's emphasis on high-stakes testing. A critique is then provided focusing on the need for an innovative solution that is not currently available, or if available, is not working sufficiently. As part of this critique, the inadequacies of currently proposed (and/or implemented) strategies are identified and contrasted to the more effective solution(s) proposed. The steps in this approach are:

- Introduce the topic and indicate your position or perspective on it
- Establish its relevance
- Show that it is a problem that needs solving
- Review the literature for solutions that have been previously tried and failed
- Critique each one and show its deficits
- Describe a novel, more interesting or workable solution

This approach can be particularly effective when writing a grant application to address an unsolved, long-standing problem of great public concern. For example, bullying and peer harassment or school-dropout prevention are two problems that are especially well suited for this approach. Both have been intractable problems of long-standing duration and have not come close to being solved or even reduced in scope — particularly with the advent of cyberbullying.

Hill previously submitted a model development grant proposal in a federal competition in which there were over 350 applications. Fifteen of these applications were funded —Hill's proposal was ranked fifth overall in this competition. This particular award came at a good time as the passage of P.L. 94-142 mandated a 180-degree turnaround in federal policy regarding how schools and other agencies were to deal with students having disabilities. These legislative and policy change(s) created a huge demand for new legal, evaluation, placement, and instructional procedures governing how these students could be accommodated and supported differently. This initial funding led to a 15- year agenda of research for Hill and his colleagues on the social integration of elementary age students having disabling conditions. It also stimulated a large number of replication studies by other investigators focused on assessing the behavioral standards and tolerance levels of general education teachers. This grant provides a great example for highlighting the importance of knowing how to frame a case argument effectively by reviewing, critiquing, and providing a workable solution to an intractable and physical, long-term problem.

Theory-Action Case Argument Approach

This method of structuring a grant is more frequently used in social sciences fields. Yet, increasingly, educational funding agencies are demanding a clear explication of the theoretical underpinnings of proposed action-based research. In this method of framing an application, a theoretical argument is conceptualized, which provides a template for action. Anticipated outcomes are linked to an enhanced understanding of the topic being addressed based on existing theories. The grant should also show how its implementation will improve policy or practice(s).

Using this approach, Sari submitted a model development grant proposal as part of a collaborative effort between a local nonprofit and a school district in the Pacific Northwest. This was a national competition hosted by the Seattle Foundation. The foundation identified only three proposals for funding.

Of more than 150 applications, Sari's proposal was fully funded to bridge the gap between lack of basic needs and in-classroom learning outcomes for inner-city middle school and high school students. This funding opportunity resulted from a pilot grant program to establish a nationwide research protocol across K-12 learning environments for increasing learning outcomes and student success rates. These awarded proposals (one in the public sector and the other in the private sector) exemplify the importance of knowing how to frame a case argument.

Key Concepts in Building Linear, Deductive Case Arguments

In this section we focus attention on the important structural elements necessary in any grant proposal, and especially including the key concepts focusing on how to build the case argument, how to support a claim, and working through an ordered set of premises. Each of these structural elements has unique features that must be carefully addressed during the grant writing process.

Building the Case Argument

We argue that there are three sets of vocabulary/concepts which you need to know to maximize your success as a grant writer. These are 1) a broad, generic vocabulary, 2) commonly used concepts and terms that exist in your field and specialization(s), and 3) the technical language required in grant writing (see Figure 17).

Broad generic vocabulary.

A broad, general vocabulary can provide a solid foundation for using language effectively. In general, the more words you have at your disposal in expressing yourself, the more options you have in communicating your precise meaning. The size and diversity of your generic vocabulary can influence your ability to conceptualize, classify, and analyze events. It is also a key determinant of how well you express yourself. Language conventions (spelling, knowledge of the rules of grammar, sentence structure, use of metaphor, etc.) are also important considerations in evaluating effective writing, but it all starts with a good working vocabulary. There are a number of strategies for building up your vocabulary. We recommend using indexes of vocabulary cards with the word on one side of the card and the correct pronunciation and definition of the word on the other. One should also develop the routine of never skipping over a word you encounter if you are not sure of its exact meaning. The dictionary is a

The size and diversity of your generic vocabulary can influence your ability to conceptualize, classify, and analyze events

Your ability to use language conventions skillfully and appropriately enhances your capacity to communicate effectively

You are responsible for knowing commonly used concepts and terms in your field, and those that refer to discredited practices

wonderful tool that should be used frequently. Free online services, such as Wiktionary[8] provide vocabulary information at one's fingertips.

Commonly used concepts and terms in your field or specialization(s).

You are responsible for knowing the commonly used concepts and terms in your field and their correct usage. For example, in the field of special education, terms such as "least restrictive environment" (LRE), "individualized education program" (IEP), "individualized family support plan" (IFSP) are all ones that have been used frequently and with which a professional in this field should be familiar. It is also important that you be aware of terms or concepts that refer to discredited practices. In the field of special education, for example, some of these concepts may include "facilitated communication," "aptitude-treatment interaction," and "learning styles." In many review panels, your positive reference to any of these labels within your proposal could spell the immediate demise of your funding chances. In short, your mastery of jargon, constructs, and terminology specific to the field about which you refer in your grant proposal can be instrumental in your ability to secure funding.

Vocabulary and concepts frequently used in technical writing of the case argument.

In the case argument process, as well as in preparing other sections of your grant application, there will be places where you may want to draw on such language conventions as *analogy, simile*, and *metaphor*. It is helpful to know the precise meaning of these conventions as they are focused on the relationships that exist among events, variables, and their language associations. Importantly, they allow you to make interesting and potentially meaningful comparisons among phenomena.

Analogy[9] transfers meaning from one source or subject to another one. It is an inference from one particular to another particular (as opposed to deduction, induction, or abduction—here at least one of the premises/conclusion is general). Analogy (e.g., arguing with some legislators about policy is like having a root canal without anesthesia!) comprises similes, metaphors, and other language forms, such as allegories, exemplification, and parables.

---

8 https://www.wiktionary.org/
9 Analogy: http://en.wikipedia.org/wiki/Analogy

Simile[10] is a figure of speech in which two unlike things are compared using connecting words such as like, as, so, than, or a verb (e.g., his resistance functioned like an invisible wall). *Metaphor*[11] is a figure of speech in which a word or phrase is used in place of another to indirectly suggest a likeness. This means it compares two objects/things without using the words like or as (e.g., given the level of attention his audience displayed, he may as well have been speaking a foreign language).

Figure 17. Knowledge development for successful grant writing

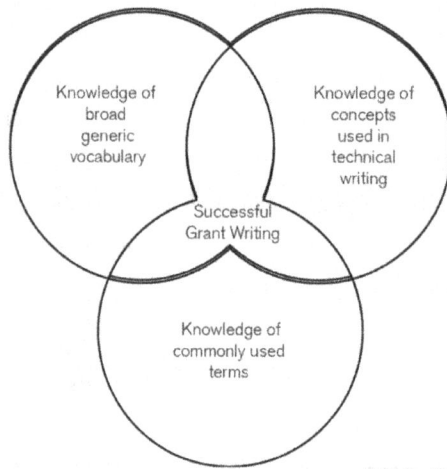

S.M.P., 2014

In building the case argument (no matter which approach is used to frame the grant proposal), you will need to use an argumentative writing style designed to support a case, a claim, or a position on a topic. It is a form of persuasion in which argument and counter argument are used to convince a reader, listener, or reviewer to accept a specific conclusion or position being promoted by an individual. In this sense, it is a form of strategic storytelling. It nearly always involves deductive logic and, sometimes, inductive argument as well. Ensure that a logical, consistent flow to the narrative wherein the argument develops progressively and the evidence cited in support of it is strong and relevant. This characteristic of progressive development of the argument is facilitated if you argue from the general case to the specific situation (i.e. the central position or claim of the case argument).

---

10 Simile: http://en.wikipedia.org/wiki/Simile
11 Metaphor: http://en.wikipedia.org/wiki/Metaphor

Another recommendation in building the case argument is that you approach this task as a two-step process. First, even before you begin writing the grant proposal, consider developing a set of *pro* and *con* arguments (i.e., for and against) in relation to a topic which interests you, or about which you are actually considering writing a grant. These arguments should focus on such questions as:

1. Is this a worthwhile topic?
2. Is it something that I am interested in doing (or that my client is interested in doing) were it to be funded?
3. What are the potential benefits and positive outcomes that would be associated with research on the topic?
4. Do I have the skills and capacity to conduct this research (or does my client)?
5. Are there colleagues with whom I can collaborate on this grant proposal?
6. How would funding of this proposal and its resulting outcomes advance my career and/or the field?
7. What are the likely obstacles and barriers that could affect implementation?
8. Does it address an important federal, state, and/or local priority?

Assuming that the pro and con arguments support developing a proposal in relation to the topic you have selected, then the next task is to thoroughly research the topic and determine its current status. As part of this process, you would be looking to identify premises that could be used to support the idea or priority defined by the topic. You should then select the approach for framing the application (e.g., strategic questions, review, critique and solve, theory-action, deductive-linear) that seems to best fit the topic or the priority in question and that you are comfortable in using. After developing a sufficient number and diversity of premises, you should determine the best way to use them within the approach you have chosen. Then arrange them in an order that works for you and that can support a smoothly flowing narrative that explicates them in the case argument.

Claims and Premises

As noted earlier, journalists (particularly syndicated columnists) are masters of the art of persuasive, argumentative writing where argument refers to making a case for something or in support of a claim. *The single, most important feature of conceptualizing and writing a compelling case argument is the careful, thoughtful, and research-based development of premises, and arranging them in a descending order according to the rules of deductive logic.*

We recommend, as a general rule, that you arrange them in a descending order going progressively from the general to the specific. Abraham Lincoln, for example, would begin thinking about the task well in advance using the systematic, deliberate style for which he was so well known in developing his major speeches, important written communications, and legal documents. His secretaries reported that when an important idea regarding a speech or document occurred to him during his daily activities, he would write it down on a scrap of paper and stick it in the brim of his stovepipe hat. When he was ready to begin crafting the document, he would assemble these scraps of paper on his desk and play with different orders for arranging them in a sequence that structured the narrative. Whether you choose to follow this system for supporting a claim, or another one of your preference, what is important is that you have a system in place every time that you write to support a claim.

We have highlighted the practice of journalists and lawyers in effectively building case arguments through clearly stated claims and well-argued, supportive premises arranged in a sequential order. As noted, having a system to support the claim, and understanding how to effectively order a set of premises become central elements in building case arguments. In general, a standard practice for ordering a set of identified premises includes:

1. Identifying the central position or primary claim that the premises are designed to support —this primary claim then becomes the last item in your rank-ordering of the identified premises

2. Rank-ordering the identified premises from first (most general) to last (most specific) —that is, the last premise prior to the statement of the primary claim

3. Carefully reading the case argument, noting where each premise occurs within the narrative and determining if it is properly placed in the sequence

It is a good idea to experiment with differing orders until you find one that seems to work best for you; then and only then should you begin the case argument writing process by explicating each premise in a narrative style of text. You will find the writing process infinitely easier if you follow this plan or a similar one as opposed to having no plan or using a trial and error method.

Arranging premises, as per above, is a combination of art and technique with perhaps more art than technique involved (see Figure 18). Basically, the final listing has to fit the need for the grant proposal (feel right and have a ring of truth). You may choose to assess your strategy by considering the following questions:

1. Is there a logical flow in the arrangement of the premises?
2. Are major and minor premises connected to each other in a
3. clear and relevant manner?
4. Halfway through the listing, would the lay reader have a good idea as to what the central position or primary claim of the case argument refers?
5. Are there the "right number" of premises to support the case argument?
6. Do these premises provide a strong logical basis or case for what will be proposed in the grant?
7. Is it a convincing argument?

There are no right or wrong answers to these questions, but they may assist you in your decision-making process.

Figure 18. Arrangement of premises

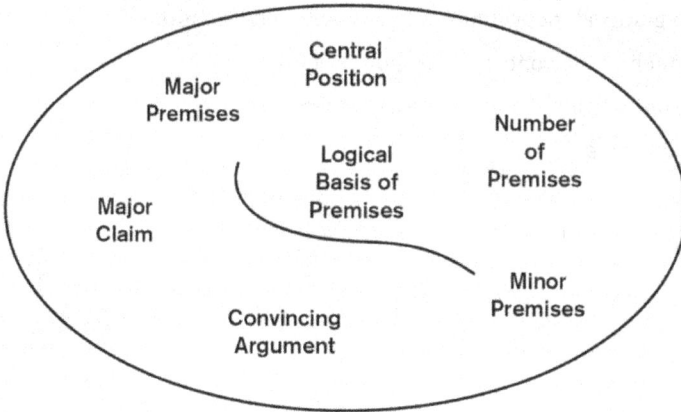

Central
Position

Major
Premises

Number
of
Premises

Logical
Basis of
Premises

Major
Claim

Minor
Premises

Convincing
Argument

S.M.P., 2014

In resorting to some "creative redundancy" here, it cannot be emphasized too strongly that you think carefully about possible alternative explanations or flaws in your argument(s) within the proposal you are developing. This is especially true within the case argument section of the proposal where flaws or alternative explanations,

suggested by reviewers, are most likely to occur, and be detected. Reviewers in general will respect you much more if you point out these potential weaknesses and deal with them yourself rather than having them do it for you. If the latter occurs, reviewers may assume you have not thought about them and judge your grant proposal negatively for your perceived lack of insight or sensitivity. By anticipating these flaws and offering a plan for correcting or explaining them (a process called "pre-correction") you protect yourself against this risk and possibly earn the reviewers' respect.

This phenomenon offers one of the very best reasons for having your proposal read and critiqued by trusted colleagues/peers before submission. They may bring perspectives to the review process that are quite different from yours and thus offer valuable insights or advice about the application that could be highly beneficial. This feedback will help you decide on the types of counterarguments you may need to consider developing in order to make the proposal as "airtight" as possible. In our experience as grant writers, we have seldom written grants alone, yet have often developed the initial draft and led much of the conceptualization process for them. We believe that grants written collaboratively are, for the most part, more likely to be superior to the ones written in full by one person.

Having trusted colleagues/ peers read and critique your proposal could offer valuable insights or advice about your application

Grants written collaboratively are, for the most part, more likely to be superior to the ones written in full by one person

Chapter IV
Understanding Funding Sources

In this chapter, we provide you with an overview of how funding sources procure and process grant proposals and we offer information on sources of funding. The purpose of this chapter is to inform you in a systemic way about options and opportunities in this context.

How It Works

In general, grant proposals seeking funding are usually processed in a similar manner by most funding sources, including federal and state agencies, national and local foundations, local government agencies, private industry, and individuals. We begin by describing the peer-review panel approach, implemented widely by federal and state agencies, and in operation within most funding sources. Significant distinctions will be identified for foundations, as well as for local and private funding processes.

Peer Review Panels

Peer review panels for judging grant applications have likely been in existence for nearly as long as has the process of procuring them. Like the jury system in the legal profession, review panels have their flaws and imperfections. To date, a better system for assisting agencies and bureaucrats in wisely investing public and/or private funds has not yet been implemented. However, there are some dynamics regarding how review panels operate about which you should know. Knowledge about these dynamics can be of substantial value to you in the preparation of your application. It is important to remember the following rule: peer review panels operate much like a jury of one's peers in that they seek solid evidence on which to base their high-stakes decisions.

Typically, a pool of professionals is identified to serve as expert reviewers who have content expertise in the area in which the grant competition occurs. This can be different for privately funded opportunities where individuals identified to serve as reviewers sometimes have no expertise or only limited knowledge and experience with the specific content of the submitted proposals (i.e., a family foundation where the board members serve as reviewers and final decision makers concerning all submitted proposals regardless of their focus). Obviously, this has direct implications for how you prepare proposals for submission to private funders as contrasted with public agencies. In this context, you must be cautious about using technical terms and jargon that may be unfamiliar to panel reviewers. In those cases where this is unavoidable, it is advisable to clearly explain and define the technical term when it is first introduced.

For federally funded opportunities, reviewers are assigned to panels typically consisting of three to five professionals along with an agency project officer. A typical grant review process employs multiple numbers of such panels where each panel is assigned a certain number of proposals to review. Proposal evaluation ratings are then standardized across panels to equalize differences that may exist among them.

As a rule, within each panel, one of the panel members is selected to chair the panel and to supervise the evaluation and deliberation processes for the panel's assigned grants. Panel members independently read, evaluate, rate and report their individual feedback to the panel chair using a common format. Panel members' ratings for each grant category (e.g., significance, design, budget, etc.) and the criteria within each one are aggregated across reviewers. The panel chair then initiates a discussion of the application and its evaluation by panel members. Often, there is a primary and a secondary reviewer for each grant application. The panel as a whole, which sometimes requires the lowering or raising of individual reviewers' ratings, ultimately reaches a consensus judgment about the application.

These rating systems, as structured as they are, can also be flawed. Sometimes, panelists bring very different rating tendencies to the panel review process. For example, once when Hill served on a three-person review panel in which group consensus was reached that a reviewed proposal was among the best they had ever seen, they were surprised by the discrepancy in quantitative ratings within their panel. On a scale of 0 to 100, two reviewers scored the proposal in the high 90s and the third reviewer scored it only in the high 70s. This low score was very discrepant with the high praise that was forthcoming from this reviewer. The reviewer confirmed that it indeed was the best application that he had seen. However, he also said it was the highest score he had ever assigned to a grant. The members of the panel managed to persuade this reviewer to raise his score substantially after reaching consensus that his score would ensure that the grant would not be funded since it projected such a wide discrepancy among the reviewers, and would lower the overall score below the funding line. This example highlights some of the vagaries of the grant submission and review process. Sometimes, in spite of your very best efforts, your grant proposal will not be funded for reasons over which you have absolutely no control. Unfortunately, these anomalies do occur from time to time, and they are examples of some of the flaws inherent in any such review and evaluation system involving human judgment. This example illustrates what is known as outlier reviews (see Figure 19).

As Professor Rob Horner of the University of Oregon has wisely noted, outlier reviews are not handled well by federal funding agencies, and most agencies have not developed policies to deal effectively with this occurrence in the grant evaluation process. Outlier reviews occur when one reviewer's ratings are highly discrepant from those of the remaining members of the panel, as in the above example. Sometimes they reflect discrepant evaluation standards across reviewers for judging a grant proposal, while, in other cases, the reviewer firmly believes the grant proposal either does or does not deserve funding while the remaining reviewers disagree. Unless this issue is addressed systematically, it almost assures that the grant will not be funded. An agency policy of discarding extreme scores and outlier reviews based upon them, and then seeking replacement reviews, would appear to be a viable strategy for dealing effectively with this problem. Yet, it is not likely that an effective solution will soon be implemented systemically for this problem.

Figure 19. Outlier review

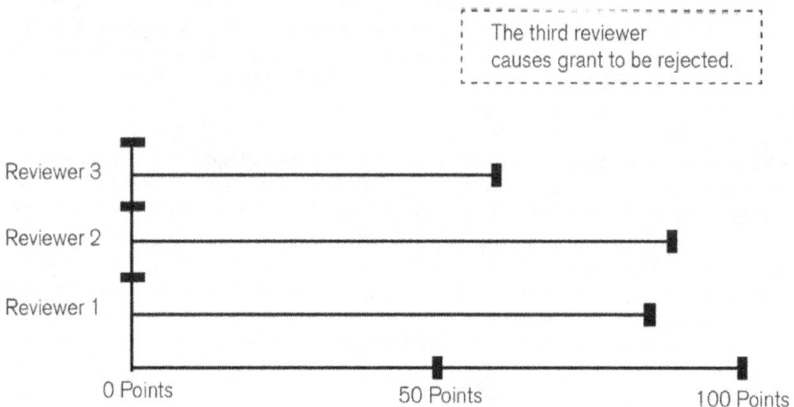

The third reviewer causes grant to be rejected.

Reviewer 3
Reviewer 2
Reviewer 1

0 Points   50 Points   100 Points

S.M.P., 2014

When a federal grant proposal is rejected for more substantive reasons and you are in a position of re-submitting for the next funding cycle, we recommend that you contact the agency project officer using a transmittal letter (also known as a précis). This transmittal letter can bring the reviewer's attention to a) what the prior panel found regarding the application, including specific disagreements among panel members about procedures or instruments, and b) the actions taken in the current application to address them. In such letters, it is important to highlight the positive findings and strengths of the application noted by the panel in the previous review. In the case of an outlier situation, you can even show how most panel members believed X or Y was a great idea and one reviewer did not. This transmittal letter alerts agency personnel to be especially sensitive to particular issues in the resubmittal's review and could enhance your chances of a positive outcome.

One has to serve on peer review panels to truly appreciate their dynamics and how panel member biases can play out in judging grant proposals. For the most part, we have found that panel members make good faith efforts to be aware of and attenuate the potential of bias in judging applications. However, there is one pervasive biasing tendency that operates consistently across reviewers and panels and that is: reviewers are more likely to have a negative mental set rather than a positive one about your proposal —or any proposal being reviewed. As a general rule, they have the expectation that your proposal is not likely to be worthy of funding even before they examine it. Hence, they typically search for flaws or reasons within the application to buttress this case or mindset. If they cannot find any or only a small number of insignificant criticisms, your proposal may have a reasonable chance to be funded.

Try to pre-correct for weaknesses or potential misinterpretations as you write your grant proposal

As we have suggested earlier in the book, a very important strategy that you can use to protect against this phenomenon is to use pre-correction methods within your proposal narrative. As you write the grant proposal, you need to think about weaknesses (real or imagined) that may exist in your application, or the possibility of misinterpretations, and try to pre-correct for them. For example, when you are building your case or reviewing and synthesizing the knowledge base in relation to your proposal's topic, you need to think of worst case scenarios involving reviewers' lack of understanding or confusion about your meaning. Other examples include the possible detection of a limitation or flaw that you have not thought about, or having information about the topic's status that you do not, and so on. If any of these occur, it could mean that your proposal is at risk for not being approved for funding. You may remember that we identified a general rule during the review process: it is far more damaging for a reviewer to point out a flaw than it is for you to recognize its possible existence and pre-correct for it. That is, you should acknowledge its possible existence within the application and take steps to prevent, buffer, or control its impact.

Some universities formally train graduate students in this review-panel approach to grant writing. For example, a colleague at a sister university who had a stellar record as a grant writer would have his students develop a small grant proposal and then arrange to have them watch as a faculty review panel evaluated and discussed each application. The review took place in a room that had audio and one-way glass in an observation chamber so the students whose grant proposals were being discussed could see and hear everything that was being said. In an effort to illustrate how peer review panels operate, panel members would deliberately misinterpret statements in the grant, demonstrate a feigned lack of understanding of what was being proposed, and go off in tangential directions that the students had no way of anticipating. The lesson being taught was that you cannot be too careful in framing your grant proposal, and you need to anticipate the possibility of reviewers making such errors in evaluating your application. In many cases, they may be as likely to do this as they are to correctly perceive and understand what you are proposing.

Some grant review processes have recently shifted to an electronic model where proposal reviewers individually evaluate and rate their assigned applications and then electronically submit their scores, which then become the focus of a conference call panel discussion. It is not clear, at present, whether or how this change in format may impact the dynamics of the panel process. Having participated in both formats of review panels, we do not find that much is appreciably changed and do not think applicants are disadvantaged by the new e-based process.

The importance of serving on grant review panels cannot be overemphasized. You will discover things about the review process that you would never learn in any other way. This experience will advantage you substantially in funding competitions if you are a keen observer and you reflect over time on what you have seen and heard about this process. There are no surefire ways of getting to serve on a peer review panel. However, being recommended to an agency's project officer by a senior researcher known to the agency is one good strategy. In the absence of such an endorsement, simply contacting the project officer assigned to a particular grant competition, communicating your request, and sending in a resume would likely be a next best strategy. For privately funded awards, there is little opportunity to serve on review panels unless you have a direct/personal relationship with the funding agency and its decision-making stakeholders. A good way to achieve this goal, other than in federal agencies, is to pursue local community organizations with wide impact, for example, The Rotary Club.

Foundations

Developing strong, working relationships with local government agencies will likely increase your proposal's chance of being funded

Some foundations that are national and international in scope, including funding agencies (e.g. United Way), are likely to follow the peer review process as described above. However, local foundations (e.g., family-owned, small) will not likely follow this process. When these foundations choose to follow a review panel process, the members serving on the panel will likely be voting stakeholders on the foundation (often family members). Depending on how close foundation stakeholders may be to its mission in the community, some family-owned and small foundations may simply have a program manager who processes grant proposals and makes decisions based on pre-defined rubrics and criteria.

These decision-making processes are also impacted by family dynamics across generations, which may determine how monies are spent and decisions made at any given moment in time. For example, during the national economic crisis that started during the first decade of this century, Sari experienced, on more than a handful of occasions, shifts in decision-making criteria of private funding sources in the middle of the proposal review process. This means that while funding sources published criteria for assessment of the grant proposals before of the submission dates, during the review process two possible scenarios may have taken place. It could be that a) family members across generations could not reach consensus on how to disburse annual funding, impacting available capacity for the year, and/or b) they received an overwhelming number of proposals and available funding capacity was limited, thus forcing them to revise their funding criteria for that cycle.

Local and Private Funding

In contrast to the review processes described above, local government agencies, as well as private/local industries and their staff, process grant proposals under a different lens. Local government agencies (e.g., cities, counties) make available and allocate financial support from three general sources: federal, state, and local funds. Local agencies usually follow a unique process in this regard depending on the community and its culture. Many cities will have structured grant application and reporting requirements. However, the decision-making process for grant proposal reviews may be ill-defined and unstructured, which could, in turn, depend on how long employees have been working in a given department or how embedded they are in the community and its systems (e.g., school districts, nonprofits). Hence, developing strong, working relationships with local government agencies (and their staff) will likely increase your proposal's chance of being funded. This applies to a small community as well as a large metropolis.

For local and/or private industry, the grant proposal-review process may or may not be a structured system. Importantly, once you have established a successful funding relationship with industry, it has the potential to continue over several years based on performance (services and available funding). For smaller businesses it could be a matter of revising the monthly or annual budget and assessing the risks and advantages associated with supporting your (your client's) grant proposal. For larger businesses (e.g., banks, corporations), an annual budgetary practice is usually in place to outline decision-making processes for evaluating grant proposals and assessing their potential funding capacity. Learning about these budgetary practices (i.e., annual budget approval) can inform your ability to submit a grant proposal just in time to ensure funding (funding cycles). The alternative, as is the case with a large percentage of grant proposals submitted to private industry, is to have your grant proposal(s) rejected based on timing — "at this time, the budget does not allow our business to entertain your proposal."

Individual funders will usually support grant proposals in an entirely different manner. While they do not formally require submission of a grant proposal packet within a certain period based on explicit criteria, they all will expect that you provide them with clear and concrete data to inform their decision-making process. For example, they may ask for P&L and BS[12] monthly/annual reports, or they may expect to see up to

---

12 P&L – Profit and Loss; BS – Balance Sheet

three years of funding history to understand the impact of the funding request at hand. Whatever the format of requested information, you need to make sure that your grant proposal (formally in writing or informally in person) contains adequate information and excels at conveying the "right" message for individual funders to act on your proposal.

Analysis and Response to RFPs

It is to your advantage to learn all you can about a funding source or target agency before submittal of your grant application. Funding agencies are required to publish and disseminate information about who they are and what they do. Most funding sources will have websites containing basic information about their mission, services, geographical impact, and funding practices/capacity. Some strategies are described below for your use in exploring and learning about funding sources. These strategies are addressed in the two next sections: 1) analyzing the funder's culture, mission and priorities; and 2) responding to RFPs.

It is to your advantage to learn all you can about a funding source before submittal of your grant application

Analyzing the funder's culture, mission and priorities.
You first need to determine the disciplinary focus area(s) in which you can a) plan and develop your career in an area of research if in academia, or b) identify a field or institution for professional affiliation and growth if in industry. Then, it is important to inspect a range of funding agencies/sources, which may have a core mission and funding priorities that match up with your own or your client's mission and values.

There are a number of strategies for accomplishing this task beginning with approaching colleagues (if in academia, other faculty and/or researchers; if in industry, other grant writers and/or development officers) who have been successful in securing funding from the agencies and sources in which you are interested. These individuals usually possess a solid repertoire of helpful information about core-mission priorities, funding dynamics, and standards that you will have to meet in order to pass muster with review panel processes.

To illustrate a point regarding quality standards, many agencies (and most funding sources) will not even review your grant proposal unless it meets certain minimal criteria (i.e., match with agency goals, proposal organization and quality, credentials of the PIs and project director, appropriate budget, and so on) as determined by the submission criteria posted (i.e., RFP process). Grant proposals in this category are called "unscoreable" and are returned to the submitting investigator(s)/organization(s) without the benefit of a panel review and its feedback. Obviously, you do not want this result. This practice a) prevents review panels from wasting precious time on non-fundable grant applications, and b) illustrates the point that funding agencies are not obligated to review each and every grant proposal that is submitted.

For federal funding agencies, another practice about which experienced investigators are familiar has to do with how review panels and the agency treat the question of nurturing a grant writer's progress in shaping and refining a promising application. Traditionally, some federal agencies allow up to two or three resubmissions of the same application to the same review panelists so applicants can incorporate reviewer feedback into subsequent iterations. This is an excellent method for teaching professionals about the required quality standards and research strategies necessary for competing successfully at the federal/national level. This system tends to result in the production of a high quality proposal and contributes significantly to the investigator's future development, which also benefits the field in which he or she works. This process is uncommon for private and local funders, though some, like foundations, may have policies in place to allow for this practice (e.g., submission of same project for funding after one or more years have passed in between submissions).

In industry, each public or private funding source (national or local) will establish a system to disseminate information about grant proposal requirements (usually posted on websites). In academia, each funding agency (i.e., public funding) publishes a core mission and a set of priorities related to that mission on its website and in other locations or venues, for example, in the Federal Register. The issuance of RFPs is the primary means that an agency uses to carry out its legislative and policy mandates. This process also justifies the agency's existence and produces statistical information for ongoing agency reports to Congress regarding the number of applications received per RFP or grant competition. It is in an agency's interest to attract as many applicants as possible in response to its RFPs. This is not the case for applicants, however, since the more applicants there are, the more competitive is the grant application process, thus lowering the baseline odds of any individual proposal being successful. The same principle applies for local and private funding. The more grant proposal applications the lower the chances of securing funding. It helps to remember this conundrum when discussing with a funding source representative or an agency project officer whether you should apply to a particular RFP (this is considered a best practice). Remember that this person will have a clear incentive for encouraging you to apply even if your chances for success are small.

The behavior or practices of organizations can be studied and analyzed to good effect in the same way that pertains to individuals. It can pay numerous dividends over a career to note carefully how agencies conduct themselves in their funding decision-making practices. For example, the Institute for Education Sciences (IES) has a mission that addresses the academic and social-behavioral performance of K-12 students. However, in its operational practices and funding decisions, IES has strongly emphasized in its RFPs and stated priorities the enhancement of academic performance and achievement. Over time, experienced investigators have determined that if one is submitting an IES application focused on social-behavioral content, it is extremely important to show how the application's outcomes will also enhance academic performance. A novice reader of the published IES material on its mission and core priorities may not have access to this critically important information. This phenomenon is a result of the agency's unique culture. Every agency has one.

It is very important to discover the nature and dynamics of how such cultures play out in funding decisions. This is another example that illustrates the relevance of developing and nurturing strong networking and collaborative skills as a successful professional/grant writer. While many agencies may not have such well-developed and powerful cultures, the point to remember is that they all develop implicit cultures that can change over time. This is true of most funding sources (i.e., human systems). Your key task is to be aware of these cultures and to understand their dynamics.

In general, local and private funding sources will not offer professional development or instructional workshops on their mission and processes, but some national and larger local foundations will offer educational opportunities for prospective and currently funded stakeholders. Federal agencies and applicant organizations (e.g., universities) may offer grant writing seminars and workshops for investigators to familiarize them with their RFP procedures and proposal requirements. It is essential that you participate in these sessions whenever possible as they can be instrumental in improving the quality and completeness of your application. Agency project officers who can respond to questions as they arise usually conduct federally sponsored seminars and webinars.

Responding to RFPs.

Just as you approach the study and analysis of a funding source or agency's core mission, priorities, and culture, you should use the same basic strategy to respond to its request for proposals (RFPs) in relation to a competition that interests you or your client. A thorough read of the published RFP is an essential first step in this regard, followed by a conversation with a project officer to answer essential questions you may have that are prompted by the RFP. Once you have completed this first step and have developed your case argument that goes under the *project significance* or *background and importance* section of the RFP, you should carefully review each section of the RFP and the instructions provided for key topics to be addressed within each.

The importance of responding to each of these topics in terms of both their letter (literal meaning) and spirit (intended or implied meaning) cannot be overemphasized. Failure to address a key topic within any section of the RFP puts your application at risk of not being funded. Most funding sources, in particular federal and state agencies, will publish RFPs that award a specific number of possible points to be earned in each section of the submitted proposal. It should be the goal of your proposal to secure as many points in each section as possible based on the RFP announcement. Local and private funding sources may refer to RFPs as LOIs (letters of interest or intent). An LOI may simply be a one to five page document that follows their criteria for funding. All advice for response to RFPs applies to LOIs, though LOIs are not usually point-based. In many instances, LOIs are the first step toward receiving an invitation to submit a proposal that responds to an active RFP.

Typically, an RFP will indicate the distribution of points across the key RFP categories and criteria within them that you must address in your application As a general rule, for research applications, these points will total up to a 100 and will usually reflect the following distribution:

- background and significance —25
- method or approach —30
- quality of key personnel —20
- local capacity, support, and resources —10
- dissemination plan —5
- budget and cost effectiveness —10

For local and privately funded RFPs or LOIs, the distribution of points across key categories will vary depending on the funding source and funding opportunity at hand. On the face of it, one would think that the larger point categories are the most important. Such is not the case. This distribution merely reflects the complexity of the material and the extent of attention and effort required to address it.

Every single point category is important, and must be addressed with the greatest effort and care. It is very important to remember that, in general, rank orders of reviewed proposals are based upon an average of panelists' individual ratings. Very often, aggregate scores for reviewed proposals are separated by tenths and sometimes hundredths of a point. To a very significant degree, the order of funding is driven by these ratings and rank orders. Thus, how well you address a small point category could have enormous impact on the likelihood of your proposal being funded.

The art of grant writing requires structure, determination, and perseverance

By now, you can probably appreciate that the art of grant writing requires structure, determination, and perseverance. Your mastery and use of the material presented in this chapter can have a powerful impact on your ultimate success in a grant proposal competition process. Very little about this process is random—it is determined instead by careful and thoughtful attention to detail.

Collaborative Proposals

Collaboration implies a reciprocal relationship suggesting that it is a cooperative arrangement among equal partners. There are a number of collaborative arrangements occurring in the context of research and grant writing such as a) you join a group of professional colleagues who are more senior and experienced than you and/or b) you work with your peers who are at approximately the same stage of professional development as you. If possible, we recommend that you seek out both forms of collaborative involvement and participate fully within them. We believe that networking and collaboration can result in increased identification of funding opportunities and enhancement of your skills as a grant writer.

The benefits of implementing "a)" above are obvious in that it affords you a significant learning opportunity, as well as the possibility of identifying one or more mentors who can be of great assistance to you as you begin your professional career. In academia, Hill served as mentor for a young professor in a partner university that had developed an effective new-faculty mentoring program. In this mentoring program, each beginning faculty member is encouraged to select a well-established professional from the field to serve as a mentor over a five to seven year period. The university seeks the mentor's agreement to collaborate with and support the faculty member in the initial stages of his or her professional career. Mentors are paid a nominal amount for their participation, but the real motivation is the development of a working relationship with someone early on in their career. In Hill's case, this particular relationship is still in effect a decade later and has produced a number of publications and grant proposals. This arrangement has worked very well for both participants in the mentor program and is a good example of productive collaborations that can occur across disciplines when there is a common set of professional interests. The learning outcomes for both parties in this instance have been very beneficial.

In industry, Sari has had the opportunity to serve as mentor to a number of young professionals interested in grant writing and fundraising efforts. As a leader of youth mentoring organizations, Sari established one-on-one educational and instructional opportunities for the development of mentoring relationships with new-to-the-field professionals. All mentees had diverse opportunities to write grants and submit proposals to multiple funding sources during their collaborations. These mentoring relationships developed over time into collaborative partnerships that resulted in ongoing professional guidance and support. The mutual learning and support resulting from these have been invaluable.

One of the benefits of this type of mentor-mentee relationship is that you are not usually competing with each other since you are at such different stages of professional development. This is obviously not the case if you choose to collaborate with peers who are in the same situation, setting, or career stage as you. The latter scenario requires sensitivity to the social impact of your own behavior as well as to the impact of others' behavior toward you. In these arrangements, it is important to give as much as you receive or at least to contribute in direct proportion to the benefit(s) you receive. The values of fairness and collegial reciprocity, not to mention trust, are some of the ingredients that are necessary for these sorts of collaborations to work effectively. Peer-to-peer collaboration is even more difficult in industry than in academia since available funding is so limited, especially in small communities. In industry, the search for funding is a very competitive and somewhat isolating journey.

Peer relationships can often be fragile and may not be sustainable in many instances. However, in our experience, they yield enormous benefits when they do work well. Importantly, the quality and productivity of our collaborations with colleagues have been positively impacted by ongoing and healthy professional relationships. It is important to note that these relationships, partnerships, and collaborations require careful and continued nurturing and a certain amount of work—as any relationship worth having does.

How to forge such mentoring relationships, particularly in an academic setting, is not always obvious. If a university has an established mentoring program for younger faculty, such as the one described herein, this is an ideal situation, yet this is not the case for most university environments. In its absence, we recommend that you approach the leader of a research unit or group whose work appeals to you and offer to volunteer your time and effort in exchange for the opportunity to affiliate with and learn from its members. We both were able to do this early in our academic careers, and it made an enormous difference in our professional development. We still have working relationships and personal associations with some of the members of our original research groups. If this sort of arrangement is not available to you (or if you are a professional in industry), then you may want to try and establish your own work group of colleagues who share common professional interests and career goals. Finally, there may be senior faculty who would be willing to collaborate with you on specific topics or projects including grant writing. Hill has been approached multiple times by younger faculty colleagues who wished to work with him on researching permutations or new applications of products (e.g. instruments, interventions) resulting from his prior research. This is an excellent way to forge collaborations leading to successful long-term working relationships. In industry, this could mean collaborating with colleagues across geographical areas who contribute to the same professional field; for example, development directors for local chapters of national organizations (e.g., YMCA, Boys and Girls Club).

When it comes to grant writing (from brainstorming ideas to conceptualizing and writing the proposal) being part of a team of trusted and talented colleagues is nearly always better than working alone. The diversity of talents, skills, and perspectives that are brought to bear and invested in this process are inevitably better than anything a single individual, working alone, can muster. Should the grant proposal be funded, then developing an agreed upon work plan that is fair and equitable is essential. It is important to explicitly develop the core strategy for this plan in anticipation of the grant proposal submission (many times, it will be part of the content of the grant proposal). It is also very important that the rewards stemming from the grant be available and distributed in a similar fashion. If you are fortunate, you may have an opportunity to participate in authorship on publications resulting from your collaborative activities or marketing of products.

Very few higher education programs provide training to advanced students in such things as professional ethics and courtesies, standards of professional conduct, and sharing. In academia, as is also the case for many environments in industry, one of the areas posing most difficulty for professionals in this context is determining authorship (i.e., ownership and attribution rights) on publications and products resulting from the funded research. Determining authorship has been a long-standing and difficult issue, particularly within academic settings, where power and status imbalances can result in the unfair treatment of participants on projects (e.g., graduate students). The urgency of this problem is reflected in the American Psychology Association's (APA) decision to address it. The APA ethics committee published a policy statement on determining authorship in 1993. This statement recommends that the decision process on this question be initiated early on in the sequence of project activities.

In our professional experience, disagreement on these issues results in conflicts and fractured relationships, sometimes lasting a life time. We have found that being pro-active and sensitive in addressing the human relationship side of the negotiation process helps to make explicit transparent communication. If in academia, we recommend collaborating with your technology transfer office early in the innovation process. Their professionals can help establish distribution systems that are equitable, inclusive, and fair. For example, as leaders of diverse organizations, we have developed sets of guidelines for determining authorship (ownership and attribution rights) among stakeholders who were involved in producing a range of products resulting from grant writing activities.

These guidelines worked very well and substantially reduced conflicts and tensions among stakeholders to solve these issues. If you are fortunate in securing funding for research that yields products that are valued by users and/or have market potential, you will almost certainly encounter this challenge.

Sources of Information about Available Funding

There are a variety of sources for information about grant support opportunities. Generic sources include libraries, institutional and higher education grants offices, subscriber information services, workshops and institutes, news media reports, requests for proposals (RFP), and announcements from federal/state agencies and private funding sources (e.g., Foundations).

There are a variety of sources for information about grant support opportunities

More specific and targeted sources are: 1) the foundation directory (foundations); 2) the catalogue of federal domestic assistance (government funding programs); 3) grants.gov (government funding); and 4) the annual register of grant support (all types). Examples of some other sources that can be useful are newsletters such as *The Educational Researcher and Education Daily* as well as publications and announcements from commercial entities like *The Grantsmanship Center News*. Another good source is *The Chronicle of Philanthropy* (online).

Most of this information is free and easily accessible via the web. You can also search through funded grants by some agencies such as on the *NIH Reporter* (http://report.nih.gov/). This option allows you to inspect the types of grants in which the targeted funding agency is interested by noting the priorities addressed by the grants they are funding. The NIH is currently setting the standard for best practices on implementation and management of awards. You may also be able to access the agency's previously and currently funded grants through this process. You are likely to find this information posted on websites of local and private funding sources.

For federally funded opportunities, we recommend that you learn how to access *grants.gov*. This resource allows you to navigate through government funding agencies and to access information on a range of topics regarding the grants process. These include: 1) how to search for grants, 2) how to find grant opportunities, 3) how to determine one's eligibility in applying for a grant, 4) how to register in order to apply for a grant, and 5) how to apply. It is an invaluable resource and guide to federal funding agencies.

For private funding, we recommend that you study local and regional opportunities. Larger private funding sources (e.g., Meyer Foundation, Seattle Foundation, Oregon

Community Foundation, Annenberg Foundation) will fund up to the scale of regional projects (e.g., West Coast). Local funding sources (e.g., family foundations, financial institutions) cater to more customized proposals that concentrate their efforts in attending to community needs. One way to do this is by conducting an online search for foundations in your state and/or city.

Chapter V
An Overview of the Foundations of Grant Writing

Takeaway Lessons and Advice

You should expect that things can and often will go wrong in the proposal development, submission, review and decision processes. Grant writing is a highly competitive, detail-driven process where dotting the i's and crossing the t's is of paramount importance. In this context, it is inevitable that there will be occasions when essential requirements will not be understood or are misinterpreted, important details will not be dealt with correctly or at all, or informal rules of the granting agency are not known or observed.

In the great majority of cases, responsibility for these errors and mistakes, resulting in a grant proposal's rejection, can be laid at the proposal developer's doorstep. This result is difficult to accept given the substantial effort, resources, and expertise that are invested in the application. However, it is usually the case that, either directly or indirectly, the investigator is accountable for this outcome.

Having said that, in this book we have described situations wherein reviewers' philosophical objections to a particular theoretical orientation or professional disagreement with the investigator about an approach described for analyzing results could cause a grant proposal to be rejected. Further, due to the psychosocial characteristics of panel members and interpersonal dynamics, it can be very difficult for the individual members of a particular review panel to reach consensus about the merits of a specific proposal.

As a general rule, if two of three panel members rate a proposal very highly and one member does not, the proposal will likely not be funded. This is the case for both public (i.e., review panels) and private funders (e.g., family members). There have also been instances, for example, in which a proposal has been highly rated in one grant competition, but does not score in the funding range. Yet, the exact same proposal (with no changes) is rated very low in a subsequent competition. Another example is when a proposal is scored within the fundable range and is not funded because higher ranked proposals consumed more of the available funds than was anticipated (a common situation during the national economic crisis).

These are all examples of developments that are not under the proposal developer's control or influence, and numerous others that fall within this same domain. When these situations occur, there is very little that can be done to remedy things or to reverse the outcome. If you lodge a complaint, you run the risk of accusing the funding agency of using improper reviewing procedures. You should only pursue this option if you have incontrovertible evidence that you have been victimized. So how does one approach addressing this problem? Our goal with this chapter is to communicate our own experience and that of colleagues in 1) how to avoid the critical errors and fatal mistakes that damage a grant proposal's funding chances, and 2) how to respond effectively when a well-developed proposal is not funded.

In contrast to the organization used across previous book chapters, we organized this material differently. We designed this format to assist you in identifying core constructs previously addressed in the book. We hope that, at the risk of being no worse than creatively redundant, our decision to revisit some of this content will be of value due to its overall relevance and because it contains important takeaway lessons for successfully managing your grant related activities.

In this chapter, there are three sections to address the topic at hand. These are: 1) research and knowledge (with four categories), 2) best practices (with six categories), and 3) interaction with funding sources (with four categories). We describe the content for each of these sections next (see Figure 20, Figure 21, and Figure 22).

1. Research and Knowledge –
Researching the Proposal Development Process and Using the Acquired Knowledge Effectively

1.1 Awareness – Becoming aware of the changed landscape of grant competitions and funding processes over the past 20 years.

1.2 Role and Impact – Determining the role and impact of funding sources via institutional and agency required assurances, along with procedural regulations affecting proposal submissions.

1.3 Study and Analysis – Understanding that the overarching mission, operations and normative practices of a granting agency can be studied and analyzed to good effect over time.

1.4   Reviewer's Critique – Using reviewers' critiques to enhance the likelihood of funding on a subsequent resubmission.

2. Best Practices –
Using Proven Best Practices in Developing Your Proposal

2.1   Proposal Review and Scoring – Enhancing the likelihood that your grant application is actually reviewed and scored.

2.2   Methodology – Ensuring that grant methods are appropriate and statistically sound and that they match the questions being asked in the RFP.

2.3   Points System – Understanding that every single evaluation category (and the available points within them) is important and that you should strive to earn the maximum available in each as funding decisions often turn on differences among applications of a point or less.

The more applications you submit to a granting agency the more likely it is you will eventually be funded

2.4   Budget Category – Realizing that, along with the category of personnel, budget is one of the most important areas for reviewers and funding sources to assess the potential cost effectiveness of a grant.

2.5   Personnel – Ensuring that 1) key personnel are qualified for the roles they are expected to perform, 2) their assigned FTE in the grant is adequate to the tasks they must perform, and 3) they are compensated appropriately given their training and expertise.

2.6   Collaborations – Realizing that when it comes to grant writing (from brainstorming and conceptualizing the proposal to its actual development), it is nearly always better to be part of a team of trusted colleagues.

3. Interaction with Funding Sources –
Understanding Reviewers and the Submission Process

3.1   Submission Process – Understanding the basics about each submission process to increase your chances of receiving awards for your proposals.

3.2   Networking – Establishing strategic partnerships to increase your proposal's chances of being funded.

3.3   Reviewers – Mapping out your knowledge about decision makers for each funding source.

3.4   Funders – Understanding the identity of the funding source and the values highlighted in each proposal.

1. Research and Knowledge –
Researching the Proposal Development Process and Using the Acquired Knowledge Effectively

Communicating clearly and precisely assumes paramount importance

At some level, the grant writing profession (when successful) can be reduced to a matter of effective communication with review panels and agency personnel. When a grant proposal is not funded, however, very often there are multiple examples of communication failure involving the grant proposal that account for an insufficient score to merit funding. Many federal grant competitions involve hundreds of applications where less than 30 are funded in the competition.

View rejection of your grant proposal as a learning opportunity to produce better and more fundable grant applications

Thus, communicating clearly and precisely assumes paramount importance. Yet, this standard is often not met. We think that a grant proposal's rejection should be viewed as a communication failure rather than as a personal or professional inadequacy of some sort. Perhaps the most important overall lesson that can be learned in this regard involves a) coping effectively with such communication failure in an attitudinal sense, b) knowing how to benefit from it, and c) turning it to one's subsequent advantage. The content of this chapter is intended to assist you in this process.

At a TEDx conference, Hill heard a health psychologist give a presentation on the importance of viewing stress within a positive or neutral cognitive frame. She described recent research that provided compelling evidence about how your attitude toward stress moderates the way it affects you. Typically, stress is viewed as negative and most people seek to avoid it. However, it turns out that if you are experiencing stress but you view stress as a potentially useful motivating factor in your life, its negative effects are powerfully muted and the impact is no more damaging than that for a person who is not under stress (McConigal, 2013). In a similar vein, we highly recommend that you view rejection of your grant proposal both as a communication failure and as a learning opportunity to produce better and more fundable grant applications.

In this section, we have identified four categories to address the topic at hand.

These are: 1.1.) awareness, 1.2.) role and impact, 1.3.) study and analysis, and 1.4.) reviewers' critique.

1.1. Awareness –

Becoming aware of the changed landscape of grant competitions and funding processes over the past 20 years.

Perhaps the most dramatic change that has occurred in this context over the past two decades is the greatly ramped up interest by professionals in securing grant funding to support projects of various types. This increased interest is true in both public and private funding areas. It is now the case that there are many more applicants for a relatively static or reduced pool of available dollars.

You have to "knock the ball out of the park"

Recently, a federal project officer was quoted as saying that in order to get funded today, "you have to knock the ball out of the park." In our view, this is essentially true regardless of the type of grant proposal you are submitting. Most importantly, it means that the overall grant writing enterprise is now much more competitive than it ever has been before —the same grant that received stellar ratings five years ago may not even score in the fundable range given today's conditions (e.g., financial capacity, number of competitive submissions). Thus, it is very likely that, "out of the box," your statistical odds of being funded are significantly lower than they were even a decade ago. When you combine that with a more competitive grant-writing environment, you must enhance both your planning efforts and your diligence in order to avoid making mistakes or errors that are under your control.

A related development in this regard has to do with the growth in standards or expectations by peer review panels regarding evaluations of the significance, scientific and practical relevance, methods, and likelihood of success of the projects they recommend for funding. Aside from the challenge of meeting these often lofty standards, one has to be concerned about reviewers raising issues that they define as relevant while the grant developer may not. This happens increasingly in today's grant writing competitions.

For example, Hill was involved in a funding competition supporting universal interventions for preventing preschool bullying with a focus on relational aggression. Though this funding agency has a primary mission of enhancing academic performance and achievement, this particular grant competition had a focus on addressing social-emotional contexts for learning, as properly addressed by the grant proposal. While the grant proposal received a good score (but below the fundable range), one of the reviewers scored it as not addressing the impact of the intervention on preschool children's academic performance. This scenario illustrates how one low score within the review panel can have a detrimental overall result for the funding of your grant proposal(s). We believe that de-contextualizing the purpose of this grant proposal from the funding agency's mission (i.e., goal for funding) resulted in an unfortunate error in judgment about the merit of the grant proposal. This is an example of a situation in which you would not want to file a complaint about this reviewer or the panel's apparent acceptance of this line of argument because the discrepancy rests on a difference of opinion.

So, what would be an alternative response to this situation? One option would be to search for another funding agency and grant competition or opportunity that would be more amenable to the focus of this grant proposal. Another (less desirable) option would be to try to make the case as this reviewer suggested and submit again. However, in doing so, one runs the risk of making a claim that would not be credible with a new set of reviewers. Alternativoly, one could assume this risk, but make the case that a universal preschool bullying intervention could possibly impact a student's school readiness, which would include the ability to engage in teacher assigned work. In our view, the first option above would be the preferred one.

Another change that has occurred, particularly in academia, involves commercialization and intellectual property management. Funded grants often provide support for products, programs, and inventions that have commercial viability and market appeal. In the field of education, for example, some products (e.g., interventions) have been developed that can generate millions of dollars annually. Particularly in the last decade, host universities for research grant awards that have developed these materials are keenly interested in owning and sharing in the licensing revenue resulting from their commercialization. Most research universities have developed protocols (e.g., intellectual property management) for the ownership and distribution of royalties from licensing of grant-produced products. In general, a portion of these funds is returned to the PI[13] and/or to the PI's research or instructional unit. What used to be a potentially lucrative enterprise and powerful motivator for individual investigators in academia has changed substantially as innovation, commercialization, and conflict of interest best practices are implemented across systems as of the 21st century.

The pressures to seek extramural funding through grants, for innovators in both academia and industry, continue to increase as local and state budgets become more and more scarce. Also, it is now much more difficult to conduct research without a funding support system that is independent of one's access to ordinarily available funds (i.e., an instructional budget for a department in a university or programming/services budget for a nonprofit). The demands of the investigative and development processes are such that they drive ever-increasing costs in time, personnel, expertise, and compensation of the contexts in which the project is carried out (e.g., a school district that participates in an innovative teacher-training project). Assessment (as measured by best research practices) of the funded project's impact and achievement of results can be defined by the implementation of research best practices, which can have a high cost.

Finally, a clear understanding of policies about the protection of human subjects participating in funded research projects and programs could be central to your success as a grant writer. Much of social science and applied research requires access to settings involving potential project participants such as families, schools, institutional contexts and so on. Funded research often involves engaging in complex negotiations with gatekeepers of the host environment for gaining access[14]. Whether your grant proposal is being submitted by a research university or by a local nonprofit/business, access to project participants can determine the success of goals as proposed in your grant narrative. Many funded intervention projects require the random assignment of students, teachers, classrooms, and/or schools to experimental and control conditions. This requirement raises a myriad of issues that must be considered in order to successfully implement a research strategy (and protect participants). Most federal funding agencies now require such randomization in experimental studies so that their results can be interpreted meaningfully and, potentially, become generalizable.

Access to project participants can determine the success of goals as proposed in your grant narrative

---

13 PI: Principal Investigator
14 This refers to research involving human subjects. Most universities, for example, have protocols in place (e.g., research compliance services) monitoring this process/interaction (e.g., Committee for the Protection of Human Subjects). These protocols inform an organization's Institutional Review Board (IRB), which regulates interaction with project participants.

However, if participants (e.g., educators, parents) do not agree to participate in a randomly assigned non-intervention control group, the applied research process could be compromised. As an alternative, many investigators offer the intervention to control group members after the original experimental group has completed the intervention. However, this option has the disadvantage of removing a comparative baseline standard for evaluating follow up effects of the intervention. For those of you who are not in academia, it is likely that expectations for the management of study participants and research-based results affiliated with your grant proposal are strongly diminished. However, it is important for you to be thoroughly familiar with your institution's policies for best practices when interacting with their clients/participants. These policies usually serve the role of an IRB[15] process in academia (e.g., confidentiality, right of refusal to participate, complaint mediation).

There are constructive, effective ways of addressing these complex issues, but they require enormous investments of time and energy. Two of the most effective investigators in this regard are Shep Kellam, M.D., (at Johns Hopkins University and a highly respected epidemiologist) and Kathleen Lane, Ph.D., (at the University of Kansas, School of Education, and one of the most successful researchers in the field of school-related behavior disorders). Their basic strategy is to a) develop a long-term, mutually beneficial relationship with the host setting's key personnel; b) demonstrate their value through consultation and technical assistance; and c) present their proposed research and activities in ways that provide a net gain or value added benefit for members of the setting. Both Kellam and Lane report that they have invested multiple years in building such relationships, which ultimately redound to the benefit of everyone. Lane has recently described her strategies for this purpose in a forthcoming publication that is highly recommended in terms of the insights it provides on this set of issues (see Walker et al., in press).

These are just some examples among many of the complex ways the grant writing landscape has changed regarding your ability to develop, submit, and manage a grant application effectively, especially if you are involved in an academic setting such as a university, college, or non-profit research institute. The underlying message of this section is that the cost of doing business in the grant writing enterprise has escalated rapidly and to levels considered unimaginable just decades ago. Thus, if you are considering a career as an investigator or a grant writer, it is essential that you know

---

15 IRB: Institutional Review Board

about and accept these burdens. Even if you are not affiliated with a research university, this section should be relevant to you when deciding to submit federally funded grant proposals because it highlights core constructs of the grant writing process.

1.2. Role and Impact –

> Determining the role and impact of funding sources via institutional and
> agency required assurances, along with procedural regulations affecting
> proposal submissions.

Over the past decade or two, the complexities of the grants process have also shown dramatic increases in the area of required assurances associated with the submission process. These changes are particularly important to understand when applying for federal funding. If your institution or organization accepts federal funds of any kind as a result of a funded grant proposal, your application will be subject to these required assurances. So aside from needing impeccable credentials that assure the principal investigator can do the proposed work well, investigators and key staff must also assure that the procedures they will implement to protect the interests and safety of human participants to be involved in the research or proposed activities meet current institutional and federal government standards and requirements. There has been a continuous escalation in the demands associated with meeting these standards in the past two decades.

In addition, due to mismanagement of awarded federal funds, individual investigators must now complete and file annually a Conflict of Interest Certification that requires working through an online instructional module on this topic. The investigator must verify lack of financial benefit or fiduciary interest in grant activities as these could be perceived as a conflict of interest. Submitting agencies can and sometimes do verify your claims regarding this certification by checking them against your federal tax return.

Finally, key personnel may now be required to complete an online module and certification process related to the prevention of workplace harassment of others. For example, colleges and universities have of late come under intense national scrutiny in relation to sexual violence on campuses that make them unsafe places for students. The federal government has just released an alarming report of the extent of this phenomenon in higher education and the report notes that, across the nation, approximately one in five students is raped during their college experience. We are likely to see much more regulation in this area down the road. If you are grant writing for industry, these regulations apply to you when a) receiving federally funded awards and b) working with children and youth (e.g., K-12 student populations), and/or families.

In addition to these assurances, most grant submitting institutions (e.g., higher education) have designated units that facilitate and process grant applications. These units perform two very important functions: a) they provide the necessary technical assistance to applicant personnel ensuring the grant meets federal, state and institutional requirements, and b) they support these personnel in completing tasks that involve institutional priorities, operations, and procedures (space issues, budget preparation, affirmative action processes, etc.). It can be the case that the investigator may not be aware or have sufficient knowledge to complete satisfactorily these tasks. Personnel in these units are usually highly skilled, and it is a very good idea to get to know them and to follow carefully the rules and advice they provide in the grant preparation and submission processes. If in industry, you will likely find nonprofit organizations offering or supporting these services[16].

In academia and most grant submitting research institutions, there will be an administrative structure in place for managing grants once they are funded. Typically, an executive administrator for research or a research and outreach coordinator will oversee this function. This person would also work closely with the host institution unit (often called the Office of Sponsored or External Research) through which the grant proposal is submitted and processed. In larger units, a business manager is usually involved as well, assisting with budget development and supervision and forging subcontracts for specialized services or external personnel, should they be required. For example, the University of Oregon's Office of Research Services and Administration (ORSA) oversees and manages guidelines for submitting grant proposals for its College of education (see Appendix B). While some of the rules and procedures of these units may seem unnecessarily bureaucratic, they all have a purpose and are quite similar across universities. It is important that you adhere closely to them in order to expedite the submission and management of your application. If you are not in academia, the likelihood is that when you submit a proposal for federal funding it will require collaboration with a research institution (usually a research university/faculty member). Hence, it is important for you to be familiar with these systems and processes.

---

16 In the state of Oregon, for example, you can access the following free-of-cost or reduced-cost services: oregonbest.org (established in more than 30 states across the country) | oregon4biz.com/SBIR | mipooregon.org

1.3. Study and Analysis –

> Realizing that the overarching mission, operations, and normative practices
> of a granting agency can be studied and analyzed to good effect over time.

Having detailed knowledge of a funding agency's mission and of its specific priorities and operational procedures can be invaluable in securing funding for your application(s). We and other experienced grant writing professionals have discovered a cardinal rule in targeting funding agencies in which we are interested: it is essential that you reference the agency's core mission in your application and show specifically how what you propose will address, support, and advance this mission.

Examples of agencies that explicitly disseminate this information to grant applicants include the Institute of Education Sciences (IES), the Small Business Administration (SBA), and the U.S. Administration on Intellectual and Developmental Disabilities (AIDD). The core missions of these three agencies are, respectively: *academic achievement and performance for IES; the commercialization and marketing of research based products for the SBA; and the enhancement of quality of life for persons with disabilities* for AIDD. We also have first-hand knowledge of rejected grant applications from each of these agencies in which reviewers noted that the application either did not address the agency's core mission or did so insufficiently. This factor was a major reason for the rejection in each instance.

It is important, but often not sufficient, to know and reference an agency's core mission and priorities. You must also be aware of its cultural ecology and values. For example, the SBA funds a granting entity called the Small Business Innovation Research (SBIR) Program. Its purpose is to translate high quality ideas and practices into innovative products that have commercial or profit-making potential. Very often, applicants for SBIR grants fail the innovativeness litmus test; that is, the applicant says it is innovative without actually making a compelling case for the practice or product's innovativeness. The impact of this scenario is different across states. In the state of Oregon, for example, only 1 in 10 SBIR grant applications are funded annually; approximately only 30% of SBIR applications are funded nation-wide[17]. In general, we have found two ways to acquire this critically important information (i.e., agency's core mission, priorities, cultural ecology, values, etc.) and to pre-correct for its absence/

---

17 You can find more information about the SBIR program here: http://www.sbir.gov/ | http:www.zyn.com/sbir/ | http://www.grants.gov/web/grants/home.html

inadequacy. One is to experience first-hand this situation (i.e., proposal rejection); the other is to learn from others who have had this experience. Thus, for example, if proposals from the SBA or any other agency that have an innovativeness evaluation category become available, we suggest you first define whether the topical area that is meaningful to your research or practice. In that case, we suggest you begin by looking at the generic literature on scientific innovation and proceed from there to document in detail how your grant idea, practice, or product meets this test. Yet another example of this values-culture-ecology phenomenon occurs within the field of developmental disabilities and the AIDD funding agency. Self-determination for persons with disabilities, or the ability to control one's life and make key choices independently, is of paramount importance in this regard. Any grant application that fails to honor this principle simply has no chance of being funded.

Federal agencies are required by law to make annual reports to Congress on their operations and progress in achieving specific goals and benchmarks. If they are also mandated to promote the implementation of specific legislation and regulations, they must also report progress on this. These reports are public documents, and they provide a treasure trove of information about the agency, its operations, barriers, and encountered obstacles along with strategies for solving problems. Such information can be extremely valuable in providing insights into an agency's operations and in developing grant applications that address its defined needs and priorities.

We have identified what can be a challenge for grant writers. For whatever reason (including chance), federal funding agencies will often end up scheduling grant competitions that come at inconvenient times for applicants (e.g., during peak vacation times, right after major holidays, within a short turnaround of the proposal from the time it is announced). Yet, on these occasions, the ratio of applicants to the number of grants that can be funded, given available funds, can be sharply reduced in favor of your grant proposal. In contrast, in competitions that occur at more typical times (spring or fall), this ratio can rise dramatically against your proposal.

The more applications you submit to a granting agency the more likely it is you will eventually be funded

Finally, many applicants who are newer to the intricacies of the grant writing enterprise become discouraged after one or two initial failures of their grant proposal(s). This is exactly opposite of the reaction that you should have. Instead, you should be thinking about submitting more rather than fewer grant applications. All other things being equal, the more applications you submit to a granting agency the more likely it is you will eventually be funded. As in baseball, the more times you are at bat, the more likely it is you will eventually get a hit. Besides, in general, skill development increases in parallel with more practice as a rule. So, this could also work in your favor.

There are a myriad of ways to research and analyze a granting agency's characteristic features to your advantage. The key is to do so in a thoughtful, analytical manner so that the resulting information can be put to effective use.

1.4. Reviewers' Critique –

Using reviewers' critiques to enhance the likelihood of funding on a subsequent resubmission.

Assuming that your grant application was competently reviewed and scored, yet was not recommended for funding, we suggest you use the reviewers' feedback, critiques, and/or suggestions as tools for making a subsequent re-write and re-application stronger. Many federal funding agencies provide space at the beginning of a re-application for this purpose, and you are expected to discuss how you responded to the reviewers' concerns/feedback. We suggest that you take advantage of this provided opportunity to strengthen your grant proposal. A major impact of this action, whether with the same or different reviewers, could result in the approval of your efforts to take the advice and use it constructively. A clear exception to this rule is a situation where a reviewer completely misinterprets what you are proposing or has insufficient knowledge and expertise to understand what you are proposing. Handling this situation skillfully is a delicate issue and, in some cases, may perhaps be best ignored.

For example, during a recent field-initiated competition, Hill and his colleagues developed an application around an early intervention to address the problem of aggression among young children. One of the reviewers' critique focused on how inappropriate the proposed design was since no reliable changes in positive outcomes have been achieved for behaviorally challenged students prior to the age of 14. This feedback was news to Hill and his colleagues since it negates the entire field of early intervention, which has a long-established range of developing early interventions having substantial efficacy. As you can grasp from this example, there will be occasions where reviewers err in judgment. If this is the case for your proposal, we suggest that you consult with experienced grant writers, researchers, and professionals who have served on review panels to inform yourself about available response to such erroneous feedback received on your proposal.

Some funding agencies will allow and even encourage you to re-submit your application multiple times with the goal of improving it to the point where it can be viably funded. In this context, the applicant and the grant proposal are both viewed as a developmental process and a work in progress. Usually, you cannot re-submit more than two or three times (depending upon the funding agency) but it is a very good thing to do and represents a great learning opportunity. When available, we strongly urge you to take full advantage of it. Again, this is mostly applicable to federally funded agencies; this re-submission process will not likely be in place for private and/or local funding opportunities.

Figure 20. Research and knowledge

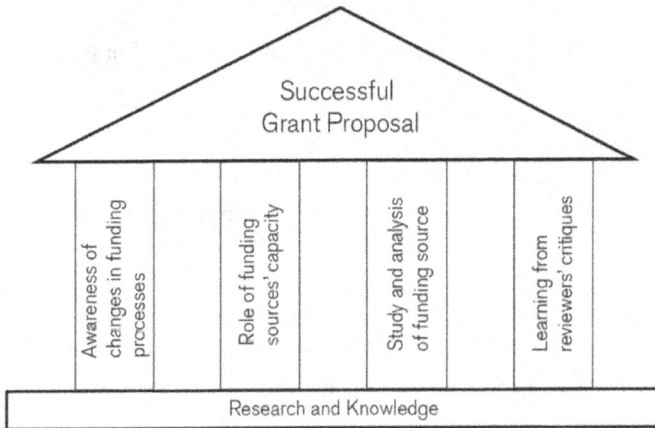

S.M.P., 2014

2. Best Practices –
Using Proven Best Practices in Developing Your Proposal

The art of grant writing involves specialized skills and careful attention to detail. In this section, we highlight some core elements for completing a successful proposal for submission, including detail-oriented aspects of the grant writing process that must never suffer, regardless of your level of expertise as a professional grant writer. In making these core elements explicit, we hope to apprise you of some expectations that funders may hold in considering your proposal/s. Your ability to address clearly and in a structured way the story told in your proposals can increase your chances of being funded.

In this section, we have identified six categories to address the topic at hand. These are: 2.1.) proposal review and scoring, 2.2.) methodology, 2.3.) points system, 2.4.) budget category, 2.5.) personnel, and 2.6.) collaborations.

2.1. Proposal Review and Scoring –

Enhancing the likelihood that your grant application is actually reviewed and scored.

One of the most discouraging experiences you can have in the grant writing enterprise is submitting an application that is not scored. This means, of course, that it was not reviewed and thus could not be scored. An application that the funding agency refuses to review means either 1) that the application was so poorly developed or "off the mark" that the funding agency deemed it not worth the reviewers' time or 2) that it did not provide the upfront, detailed information that the funding agency requires of all applicants.

To address item one above, you have to develop the highest quality application of which you are capable and do your best to align it with the objectives and priorities of the grant competition. Typically, funding agencies do not indicate specifically why they refuse to review an application, but if it involves item one, then it clearly does not meet the funding agency's standards. Item two is much more easily addressed. In most federal funding competitions, detailed information on the applicant organization and federal requirements associated with the competition are requested. Many applicants approach this part of the grant proposal casually and often pay a penalty for doing so. The funding agency will be disinclined to overlook missing or error prone information in this section of the application, which can result in a refusal to review and score it. This outcome is highly preventable and speaks to the importance of carefully dotting all i's and crossing all t's in the grant proposal —even in areas of the RFP that are only tangentially related to the actual grant.

2.2. Methodology –

Ensuring that your grant methods are appropriate and statistically sound and that they match the questions being asked in the application.

The methods section of a grant proposal is also a highly vulnerable area by which many applications are rejected. If you are preparing a research application and you are unsure of your expertise in this regard, it is imperative that you seek expert input in both the design and analysis procedures you plan on using. This includes evaluation and assessment of impact as described in the grant proposal. Further, these procedures must be appropriate for the questions you are proposing to investigate. Increasingly, peer review panels have one or more members (e.g., biostatisticians) who have very high levels of expertise in these areas, and it is difficult to pass the bar that they establish.

If your application does not have a research focus, then the challenge of preparing a solid methods section is less daunting. Basically, your task is to convince the reviewer you know what you are doing and that the procedures and strategies you are proposing will pass the tests of feasibility and acceptable professional practice. However, you should keep in mind that if your method(s) are judged negatively in the review process, your grant proposal will not likely be funded.

2.3. Points System –

Understanding that every single evaluation category (and the available points within them) is important and that you should strive to earn the maximum available in each as funding decisions often turn on differences of a point or less among applications.

This observation is re-addressed here due to its extreme importance to a successful funding outcome. Throughout our careers, we have participated in numerous grant competitions involving sometimes hundreds of applicants. Typically, 20 to 30 or so grant proposals are actually recommended for funding out of this pool. Summary scores are derived for each application by aggregating scores across individual reviewers to arrive at a summary score for the grant proposal. This score can go up or down depending upon how the panel discussion of the application goes. In general, this is accomplished through adjustments to the scores of individual reviewers (with their consent) and then re-calculating a total score, which is then used as a basis for rank ordering the top proposals in the competition.

As a rule, the evaluation categories used by reviewers to award points to a potentially federally funded grant proposal total 100. In a competition involving hundreds of applicants, the difference between a funded and unfunded proposal can literally be one point or less. Thus, a four-point evaluation category for dissemination activities, for example, could make an enormous difference in your grant proposal's fate if you received an average score of two instead of four. Thus, you must make it a standard practice to get the maximum number of available points in each evaluation category.

It should be noted here that there are caveats and exceptions to every seemingly ironclad rule. For example, even when you do everything right and achieve a total score and a rank order position in the fundable range, you still may not be funded. This occurs when the funding agency sets a cutoff score for funding and/or runs out of money before agency personnel get to your grant proposal, as they typically go down the rank order list until funding is exhausted. This process, in general, also applies to private and/or local funding. This is very discouraging when it happens and it has happened to us more than once. All you can do is resubmit and hope for a different outcome the next time. However, if the funding agency should serendipitously discover some additional funds to add to the competition, PIs and lead investigators of the next list of highest ranked unfunded proposals will be contacted according to their respective rank orders.

2.4. Budget Category –

Realizing that, along with the category of personnel, budget is one of the most important areas for reviewers and funding sources to assess the potential cost effectiveness of a grant.

The budget has to be
pristine in its
accuracy and all
calculations must be
done correctly

Budget is the category of your grant proposal where reviewers and the funding agency make a judgment about the cost effectiveness of your application and whether to invest in it. In terms of mechanics, the budget has to be pristine in its accuracy and all calculations must be done correctly.

Your budget should
never exceed
the award level
recommended by the
funding agency

We recommend that you involve your unit's business manager, budget analyst, or accountant in developing the budget once you have decided on the type and amount of resources required to carry out the grant satisfactorily. If not in academia, your organization may or may not have access to this expertise on staff; therefore, you must network and collaborate with a larger system (e.g., if in a nonprofit, available expertise may be accessible from the city, the county, or from available board members).

On this note, you must never submit a budget amount in a grant competition that exceeds the funding level recommended by the funding agency. A sample budget spread sheet from a grant application is included herein (see Appendix C) to illustrate how a typical budget format for a multi-year award looks (federal funding). As a rule, the grant application packet will provide a budget template for use in completing this task. Some funding agencies will allow for your own design of a budget template, as long as it includes and accurately displays all required information.

Your budget has to pass muster for accuracy, completeness and reasonableness. That is, the funding agency and reviewers must see it as competently put together and as feasible when cast against what you plan to do with the funds in the grant. How they respond to your proposal's budget is an important part of their overall evaluation of you as a principal investigator (if not in academia, as a representative of your organization).

2.5. Personnel –

Ensuring that a) key personnel are qualified for the roles they are expected to perform, b) their assigned FTE in the grant is adequate to the tasks they must perform, and c) they are compensated appropriately given their training and expertise.

Despite the significance of budget and cost effectiveness to a successful grant application, it pales in comparison to the importance of the expertise of a principal investigator and key implementation staff. As noted previously, fully half of all grants are rejected because of concerns about the expertise of grant personnel —especially the proposed project director (PI). Thus, if there is a lack of expertise or a mismatch between grant-assigned roles and the expertise of the person occupying the role, there is little chance your grant proposal will be funded.

A second critical issue has to do with the amount of time the PI can devote to the role. It cannot be too little or too much. As a rule, a PI should have no less than .20 FTE assigned to directing the funded project, with adequate staff in supporting roles such as coordinators, supervisors, clerical, technical, and so forth. One should avoid planned Co-PI leadership roles unless there is a compelling reason for proposing such an arrangement. Both reviewers and funding agency personnel tend to see such shared decision-making and joint responsibility as risky. Finally, the salary compensation of personnel assigned to differing project roles should be reasonable and reflect prevailing salary ranges for each position. Personnel will be your most expensive budget category and requires careful thought regarding cost effectiveness so you maximize your available dollars up to the funding level indicated by the funding agency.

2.6. Collaborations –

Realizing that when it comes to grant writing (from brainstorming and conceptualizing the proposal to its actual development), it is nearly always better to be part of a team of trusted colleagues.

There are very few situations in the grant writing development process where one person's individual efforts can match those of a trusted, compatible group of colleagues with shared expertise and vision. This has been invariably true in our respective experiences with grant writing. However, it is a more difficult management process as you have to negotiate carefully individuals' proposed project roles and responsibilities, give professionals due credit for their ideas and contributions, assign grant development tasks appropriately, develop a plan for sharing resources from the grant if funded, and manage ideation-to-proposal submittal team time within the RFP deadlines.

For example, Sari managed the development of an RFP funded by the US Department of Education. A total of five higher education institutions and one nonprofit organization were represented, with up to two individuals per institution. The process from ideation to submission of the grant proposal took over four months. During this time, Sari (project manager) convened weekly or bi-weekly meetings, as necessary; facilitated two all-day working retreats; and produced all meeting agendas, minutes, and revised versions of the grant proposal through the working process. Managing collaborative grant writing projects can be challenging, yet it can also be greatly rewarding. In Sari's case, all project participants developed close relationships that turned into long-lasting friendships and professional support networks. We firmly believe that our collaborative grant experiences have been more valuable and rewarding than our solitary ones.

Figure 21. Best practices

RFP	Enhancing chances for proposal to be reviewed and scored	Strong grant proposal
	Use of statistically-sound methods.	
	Striving to earn the maximum available points.	
	Accurate budget to assess cost effectiveness.	
	Qualified and properly compensated personnel.	
	Producing collaborative proposals.	

S.M.P., 2014

3. Interaction with Funding Sources – Understanding Reviewers and the Submission Process

In general, this section focuses on private funders as a way to highlight content that has been included across all chapters of this book. By developing a clear understanding of expectations, identity, process, and relationship-building opportunities relative to funding sources, you may increase your capacity to sustain a career as a successful grant writer.

Today, supplementing federal/state funding with private funding (e.g., Foundations, individuals, businesses) is more relevant than ever. In academia, for example, there are research units and programs that used to receive more than twenty federal awards annually for more than a decade, yet in this economy, those have reduced to a handful of awards. Hence, strategic storytelling to secure awards from private funders should be at the forefront of your agenda as a grant writer. Your ability to comprehend the importance of developing strong relationships with private funders could determine your overall success rate as a grant writer.

In this next section, we have identified four categories to address the topic at hand. These are: 3.1.) submission process, 3.2.) networking, 3.3.) reviewers, and 3.4.) funders.

3.1. Submission Process –

Understanding the basics about each submission process to increase your chances of receiving awards for your proposals.

There is no substitute for a brilliant idea around which to build a grant application

Improving your skills as a storyteller will increase your capacity to secure awards

There is no substitute for a brilliant idea around which to build a grant application. The best ideas involve proposing solutions to pressing, unsolved problems, or solutions that address clear gaps in the existing knowledge base. Note that even though brilliant, your ideas and proposals may not be funded. Even when you do everything. right, when the funder sets a cutoff score for funding and/or runs out of money, your chances of getting funded may decrease significantly. This is very discouraging when it happens. All you can do is resubmit and hope for a different outcome the next time. The goal is to develop as many quality applications as you can in order to maximize your chances over time and across your career.

As a general rule, apply for the average announced award amount of the grant. The budget section of your proposal is as important as the narrative. Some funders will allow for your own design of a budget template, as long as it includes and accurately displays all required information. We suggest that you show how the allocation of a grant to your proposed research or program is a better investment of funds than what exists or what has been tried in the past. When approaching private funders, you will benefit from understanding that resubmissions of the same application to the same funder are very uncommon.

When submitting a proposal for federal funding, if in industry, you will likely be required to collaborate with a research entity (e.g., university, faculty). In the case of higher education institutions, they are likely to have units that facilitate and process grant applications providing the necessary technical assistance to applicant personnel. These practices are in place to ensure the proposal meets all requirements before submission. It is important for you to be familiar with these administrative structures and processes. We recommend that you involve the proposing unit's business manager or budget analyst in developing the budget for your proposal. If you and/or your organization do not have access to this expertise, network and collaborate with a larger system (e.g., City, County). If grant writing for industry, you can access free-of-charge services to supplement some of this expertise from organizations like oregon.best.org, for example (established in more than 30 states across the US).

It is now the case that there are many more applicants for a relatively static or reduced pool of available dollars. Therefore, your statistical odds of being funded are significantly lower than they were even early during the first decade of the 21st century. As a grant writer, you must enhance both your planning efforts and your diligence in order to avoid making mistakes or errors that are under your control. Improving your skills as a storyteller as you work through the logistics of the submission process, will increase your capacity to secure awards.

Today, funders establish systems to disseminate information about grant proposal requirements by posting information on line. Most of this information is free and easily accessible via the web. Both federal/state and private funders will post RFPs for use by applicants in the proposal development and submission process. Smaller private funders (e.g., local family foundations) will likely post LOIs or steps for the process of submission. An LOI may simply be a one to five page document that follows their criteria for funding; these are usually not point-based. Remember that failure to address a key topic within any section of the RFP and/or LOI puts your application at risk of not being funded. As a professional grant writer, you must develop a clear understanding of funding cycles for industry. These are usually posted on their websites (e.g., financial institutions).

3.2. Networking –

Establishing strategic partnerships to increase your proposal's chances
of being funded.

Networking can result in increased identification of funding opportunities and enhancement of your skills as a grant writer. Successful networking will require that you approach colleagues (e.g., grant writers, development officers) who have been successful in securing funding from the funding sources in which you are interested. These individuals usually possess a solid repertoire of helpful information about core-mission priorities, funding dynamics, and standards that you will have to meet in order to pass muster with review panel processes.

Peer-to-peer collaboration is difficult in industry since available funding is so limited, especially in small communities. This competitive search for funding can make your grant writing experience somewhat of an isolating journey. Peer relationships can also be fragile and may not be sustainable in many instances. However, in our experience, they yield enormous benefits when they do work well. It is important to note that they require careful and continued nurturing and a certain amount of work — as any relationship worth having does.

Establish your own work group of colleagues who share common professional interests and career goals. This could mean collaborating with colleagues across geographical areas who contribute to the same professional field (e.g., development directors in local chapters of a national nonprofit). Consider collaborating with school districts and other agencies in developing consortium grants. This will most likely result in a strong and unique proposal. Local chamber of commerce could also be a source of assets and networking opportunities.

Establish your own work group of colleagues who share common professional interests and career goals

Keep in close communication with local agencies (e.g., foundations, philanthropic organizations), government (e.g., city, county), and higher education institutions (e.g., universities, colleges) to gain common language and facilitate discourse about pressing issues that could lead to successfully pursuing funding. Connect with the funding agencies in which you are interested to be a reviewer and figure out ways of staying current with their giving priorities. You can start doing this by calling people on the phone to network with them and then nourishing the relationships until they become part of your grant-writing ecosystem. Remember that when it comes to private funders, there is little opportunity to serve on review panels unless you have a direct/personal relationship with the funding agency and its decision-making stakeholders. For example, you could become a voting Board member.

You could also become a member of a local club, like Rotary, which makes funding available to its community. This could give you an opportunity to participate as member of a review panel to decide which proposals are funded and why.

3.3. Reviewers –

Mapping out your knowledge about decision makers for each funding source.

Local foundations (e.g., family-owned, small) will not likely follow a review panel process. The members serving on the panel will likely be voting stakeholders in the foundation (often family members). In some cases, the reviewer might be one individual instead of a panel. Depending on how close foundation stakeholders may be to its mission in the community (e.g., first generation vs. fourth generation family members), some local foundations may simply have a program manager who processes grant proposals and makes decisions based on pre-defined rubrics and criteria. Reviewers sometimes have no expertise or only limited knowledge and experience with the specific content of submitted proposals. It will be your job to provide them with a clear mental picture of the proposed project through effective storytelling.

These decision-making processes are also impacted by family dynamics across generations, which may determine how monies are spent and decisions made. Through the submission, competition, and/or funding processes, funders may revise their funding criteria for that cycle based on family members not reaching consensus on annual distribution of funding, or for having received an overwhelming number of proposals in relationship to available funding capacity, or any other reason.

The grant review process may or may not be a structured system. For example, for smaller businesses it could be a matter of revising the monthly or annual budget and assessing the risks and advantages associated with supporting your proposal. For larger businesses, an annual budgetary practice is usually in place to outline decision-making processes for evaluating grant proposals and assessing their potential funding capacity.

3.4. Funders –

Understanding the identity of the funding source and the values highlighted in each proposal.

Local government agencies, as well as private/local industries and their staff, process grant proposals under a different lens. Local government agencies (e.g., cities, counties) make available and allocate financial support from three general sources: federal, state, and local funds. Local agencies usually follow a unique process in this regard depending on its community and its culture. For example, many cities will have structured grant application and reporting requirements, while the decision-making process for grant proposal reviews may be ill-defined and unstructured. This could be influenced by how long employees have been working in a given department or how embedded they are in the community and its systems. Hence, developing strong working relationships with local agencies (and their staff) will likely increase your proposal's chance of being funded. This applies to small communities and large metropolis.

Individual funders may not formally require submission of a grant proposal packet within a certain time frame and based on explicit criteria. Yet, they all will expect that you provide them with clear and concrete data to inform their decision-making process to fund a proposal. We recommend that you study local and regional opportunities as you analyze opportunities for funding. Individual donors and local foundations will expect you to master current conditions in the socio-cultural-economic landscape of your community and reflect their impact within your proposal (e.g., crime recidivism, economic development, promotion of education).

In general, local and private funding sources will not offer professional development or instructional workshops on their mission and processes, but some national and larger nonprofits (e.g., foundations) will offer educational opportunities for prospective, as well as actively funded stakeholders. Study and analyze the agencies that you target for grant applications. You could do so in much the same way in which you would research literature in a topic of interest. Agencies operate off both public (formal) and sub-rosa (informal, not published) rules. You need to be familiar with both sets of rules. You could do this by establishing working relationships with fun/program managers at these agencies.

Affiliate with an organization which holds similar values and views to yours

As a professional grant writer, we suggest that you asses the importance of establishing a meaningful affiliation with an organization which holds similar values and views to yours. This decision could help ensure that your passion and commitment drive your grant-writing process. Assess your capacity and match the content of your proposal with your funder's needs and values. Do so in a transparent manner, without forcing either your or their values onto the proposed project for funding. A primary reason for private sources not funding a proposal stems from an existing gap between the proposed project and the funder's values and mission. It is essential that you reference the agency's core mission in your application and show how what your propose will address, support, and advance this mission.

Figure 22. Interaction with funding sources

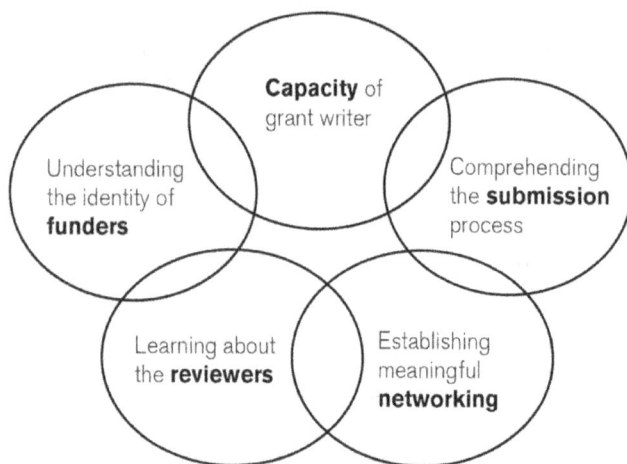

Capacity of grant writer

Understanding the identity of **funders**

Comprehending the **submission** process

Learning about the **reviewers**

Establishing meaningful **networking**

S.M.P., 2014

Critical Lessons about Grant Writing

We have identified eight critical lessons to keep in mind as you write grants:

- Lesson One: *The reviewer's initial impression of your proposal is often established in the first few pages of the narrative.* Negative impressions are quick to formulate while positive impressions develop gradually over time as the reviewer acquires more information about you and the proposal in order to form a final judgment. Even the first page could make the difference as to whether your proposal will be considered for funding.

- Lesson Two: *If the initial case argument for what you are proposing is not clear, straightforward, and compelling, the chances for your proposal being funded are remote.* Typically, reviewers make up their minds about this issue within the first five to ten pages of the proposal. If the initial argument is not persuasive and does not fully engage the reviewer, your proposal will likely not be considered for funding.

- Lesson Three: *The grant-writing process involves the skillful use of both deductive and inductive forms of logic —you need to study and master them both— in addition to clear, fluent use of language.* Assume that your readers will not have mastery over the content of your proposal. How you express your proposal in writing can define your ability to secure funding. Make sure that your proposal (formally in writing or informally in person) contains adequate information and excels at conveying the "right" message for individual funders to act on your application.

- Lesson Four: *Remember that, in general, the more applications you submit the more likely it is you will eventually be funded.* We suggest that you use feedback from rejected proposals to learn and improve your grant writing skills.

  > *The more applications you submit the more likely it is you will eventually be funded*

- Lesson Five: *Have a clear understanding of depressed environments, urgent needs, or gaps in the service system/s in which you are embedded.* We recommend that you also understand potential solutions that will maintain public interest beyond the urgent need at hand.

- Lesson Six: *Assume that expectations for the proper management of human participants, services, and research-based results affiliated with your proposal will be high and must be adhered to closely.* Be familiar with your institution's policies for best practices when interacting with participants in funded projects (and in general). For example, these policies could be about confidentiality in the work place, right of refusal to participation, complaint mediation, etc. Once funded, key personnel may now be required to complete online modules and certification processes related to the prevention of workplace harassment of others, as well as proficient financial management. You are likely to see ongoing regulation in these areas when receiving large awards, working with children and youth, and/or families.

- Lesson Seven: *There can be no avoidable errors in the proposal narrative.* Proposals that are replete with avoidable errors in grammar, mistakes in responding to RFP instructions or guidelines, and the failure to address key topics, tasks or questions in developing the document are very unlikely to pass muster with peer review panels.

- Lesson Eight: *Ensure that you have the support of your applicant organization and that it has the demonstrated capacity to host the project.* When you do so, you are increasing your proposal's strength by securing that the project can achieve its stated goals.

Concluding Remarks

In this review chapter, we have focused on trying to give you the benefits of our experience and that of others in the grant writing profession. There are a number of "takeaway lessons" herein that we hope will be of assistance to you whether you choose to use grant writing as a tool in your professional activities or you decide to pursue an actual career in grant writing. Effective grant writing is not a science in our view, but rather is a form of craftsmanship that has artistic elements. It can be learned and mastered by a broad range of individuals who bring diverse skill sets to this process. As we have noted, you get better at it with practice.

Your proposals are only as good as your last funded grant; you need to keep improving on your skills

Take time to train others about the grant writing process and how to develop their grant writing skills

It is also very important to remember: "your proposals are only as good as your last funded grant." The message behind this observation should keep you from thinking you have ever completely mastered the grant writing process and that there is no need to keep improving on your skills. It is also a reminder that it is very important to strive to write the very best grant proposal you can every single time regardless of the circumstances.

A great way to keep your grant writing skills sharp so that you continue to be a successful grant writer is to take the time to train others about the grant writing process and to educate them on how to develop their grant writing skills. In our experience, we know that "practice makes perfect." Whether you choose to write grants within academia or industry, the content included in this book is designed to help you improve your skills as a professional. If you liked this book, tell your friends and colleagues. Thank you for reading!

Foundations of Grant Writing

A systemic approach based on experience.

Walker, H.M., & Pascoe, S.M. (2015)

Copyright © by the University of Oregon

Appendix A: Recommended Readings

We recommend to you the works of Rudolph Flesch on expository writing and his extensive commentaries on how to write, speak and think more effectively. Flesch has contributed over 20 books on writing, reading, and speaking. He is arguably the most influential figure of the last 50 years on professional writing for clarity and readability. A simple Google search reveals

Both readability and clarity are essential skills to master in grant writing

his prolific contributions on this topic. He is the author of Why Johnny Can't Read and What You Can Do About It. Flesch has written a most important, now-classic book called, The Art of Readable Writing, containing some of the best essential rules and conventions on effective writing that we have seen. It is highly recommended that you consult this classic work on effective writing. Hill has used Flesch's contributions extensively in his teaching of graduate courses in how to do effective grant writing and found them to be an invaluable resource. Another highly recommended book by Flesch is, How to Write, Speak and Think More Effectively; its content is timeless and the book can be accessed easily.

We also recommend that you get familiar with the work of Michael Wells, who is principal consultant for Grants Northwest. He is a prolific published author in the topic of grant writing and consistently offers literature reviews of the most relevant titles for grant writers. You can see a sample of his reviews here:

http://www.grantsnorthwest.com/resources/recommended-books/. For example, his book Grant Writing Beyond the Basics 3: Successful Program Evaluation assists the reader to embrace evaluation and incorporate it in an organic way into the grant writing process, which will strengthen a proposal. His easy-to-read materials and research-based content is informed by decades of grant writing experience. This approach makes the reading of his materials and recommended titles a worthwhile experience.

You will find in the bibliography section of this book resources to the following authors who we recommend that you read: Flesch, Moore, Luntz, and Wells. We have found that their work can be instrumental in informing your experience as a grant writer.

Appendix B: ORSA Form (sample)

APPLICATION SUBMISSION REQUEST

NOTE - our internal Electronic Proposal Clearance System record MUST be finalized 3 business days PRIOR to published deadline.

Funding Source	
Specific Program (if applicable)	
Specific Goal (if applicable)	
Program Guidelines URL	
CFDA # or Opportunity #	
Deadline	
Is this a grants.gov submission?	
Is this an NSF fastlane submission?	
Is UO the prime applicant?	
If not, who is the prime applicant?	

Title	
Proposed start date	
Proposed end date	
Project type	
Number of years	
Maximum amount of award	

Geographical Area of impact	

PI Name	
Co-PI (if applicable)	
Are there other key personnel?	
If yes, please list	

Will there be subcontracts?	
If yes, please list	

Human Subjects?	

What type of research is this? (choose 1 from below)	
Basic Research	
Applied Research	
Development	

Appendix C: Budget Spread Sheet (sample)

FIVE YEAR R&R DETAILED BUDGET								YR 1	YR 2	YR 3	YR 4	YR 5	TOTAL
PI DEPT: *(or name of principal investigator)*							Start						
Name of Research Institution/University							End						
PERSONNEL SALARIES/WAGES	*Institution*	*SALARY*	*Yr 1*	*Yr 2*	*Yr 3*	*Yr 4*	*Yr 5*						
for AY 9-mo. and 12-mo appts.	*APPT.*	*BASE*	*%*	*%*	*%*	*%*	*%*						
Names	*12*												
PERSONNEL	*Institution*	*SALARY*	*Yr 1*	*Yr 2*	*Yr 3*	*Yr 4*	*Yr 5*						
Summer salaries for 9-mo. appts.	*APPT.*	*BASE*	*%*	*%*	*%*	*%*	*%*						
Names	*9*												
*GTF I and GTF II (Full Time Tuition)	*UO*	*SALARY*	*Yr 1*	*Yr 2*	*Yr 3*	*Yr 4*	*Yr 5*						
GTF Salaries	*APPT.*	*BASE*	*%*	*%*	*%*	*%*	*%*						
GTF AY effort													
GTF summer effort	*– leave blank –*												
		Total Academic Terms											
		Total Summer Terms											
		Total Salaries & Wages											
PERSONNEL FRINGE BENEFIT (OPE)													
Benefits for AY 9-mo. and 12-mo appts.													
Names													
PERSONNEL FRINGE BENEFIT (OPE)													
Summer benefits for AY 9-mo. and 12-mo appts.													
Names													

(continued)

FIVE YEAR R&R DETAILED BUDGET

				YR 1	YR 2	YR 3	YR 4	YR 5	TOTAL
GTF, 1% + insurance/fees			1%						
Total Fringe Benefits									
TOTAL PERSONNEL									
SUPPLIES									
List									
Total Supplies									
EQUIPMENT (>$5000/unit)									
List									
Total Equipment									
TRAVEL									
Domestic									
Foreign									
Total Travel									
SUBCONTRACTS									
[Total costs, subcontract Institution 1]			<=25K						
			<25K						
Total Subcontracts									
PARTICIPANT SUPPORT									
Stipend									
Travel									
Substinence									
Other									
Total Participant Support									
OTHER									
Graduate Tuition & Off-Site Facility Rental (F&A Exempt)									
Academic Year Graduation Tuition									
Summer Graduation Tuition									
Rental Costs of Off-Site Facilities									

(continued)

FIVE YEAR R&R DETAILED BUDGET

				YR 1	YR 2	YR 3	YR 4	YR 5	TOTAL
OTHER									
Consultants									
[Other]									
Total Other									
TOTAL DIRECT COSTS (includes Total Subcontracts Costs)									
MODIFIED TOTAL DIRECT COSTS (MTDC)*									
List									
– Enter Applicable F&A Rate Below –									
Facilities/Administrative Costs (F&A) **of MTDC**									
Domestic									
TOTAL COSTS				F&A?	F&A?	F&A?	F&A?	F&A?	
(TOTAL COSTS + F&A)									

*GTF = tuition covered and stipend students

Includes Annual increase on UO Personnel of 5.0% (1.5% on GTF salary), 8% on GTF Fees, 6% on Insurance, and 9% on GTF Tuition, 2.12% COLA on Non-personnel costs. 2 CFR §200.68 Modified Total Direct Cost (MTDC).

*MTDC means all direct salaries and wages, applicable fringe benefits, materials and supplies, services, travel, and subawards and subcontracts up to the first $25,000 of each subaward or subcontract (regardless of the period of performance of the subawards and subcontracts under the award). MTDC excludes equipment, capital expenditures, charges for patient care, rental costs, tuition remission, scholarships and fellowships, participant support costs and the portion of each subaward and subcontract in excess of $25,000. Other items may only be excluded when necessary to avoid a serious inequity in the distribution of indirect costs, and with the approval of the cognizant agency for indirect costs.

Bibliography

Behrens, L. (2001). *Making the case: An argument reader.* Upper Saddle River, NJ: Prentice Hall.

Center for Nonprofit Advancement (2012). Snapshot of economy's impact on nonprofits in greater Washington. Washington, DC: Center for Nonprofit Advancement. www.nonprofitadvancement.org

Flesch, R. (1963). *How to write, speak and think more effectively.* New York, NY: Signet (Penguin Group, USA).

Flesch, R. (1985). *Why Johnny can't read and what you can do about it.* New York, NY: Harper & Row, Publishers, Inc.

Flesch, R. (1994). *The art of readable writing.* Hoboken, NJ: Wiley & Sons, Publishing.

Jagpal, N. and Laskowski, K. (2011). The state of general operating support report and the state of multi-year funding report. Washington, DC: NCRP. www.ncrp.org

Luntz, F. (2007). *Words that work: It's not what you say, it's what people hear.* New York, NY: Hyperion.

McConigal, K. (2013). How to make stress your friend. TEDGlobal. http://www.ted.com/talks/kellymcgonigal_how_to_make_stress_your_friend

Moore, B. (1995). *Making your case: Critical thinking and the argumentative essay.* London, UKI: Mayfield Publishing Co.

Moore, B., and Parker, R. (2012). *Critical thinking.* New York, NY: McGraw-Hill.

Network for Good (2013). The Network For Good Digital Giving Index. http://www1.networkforgood.org/digitalgivingindex#OGS124 *Foundations of Grant Writing*

The Nonprofit Association of Oregon et al. (2012). Oregon nonprofit sector report. The state of the nonprofit sector in Oregon 2011. Portland, OR: The Nonprofit Association of Oregon. www.nonprofitoregon.org

Pascoe, S.M. (in press). Nonprofit management of change. CINCO: Principles for organization-wide change. University of Oregon. Eugene, OR: UO.

US Department of Education (2012). Digest of education statistics. Washington, DC: National Center for Education Statistics, Institute of Education Sciences. http://nces.ed.gov/programs/digest/d12/

Walker, H. M. (2012). *Preparing fundable grant proposals: A roadmap for professionals. University of Oregon.* Eugene, OR: UO

Walker, H. M., Forness, S. R., and Lane, K. (in press). *Design and management of scientific research in applied school settings.* In B. G. Cook, M. Tankersley, & T. J. Landrum (Eds.), Advances in learning and behavioral disabilities (Vol. 27). Bingley, UK: Emerald Group Publishing Limited.

Wells, M. K. (2014). *Grant writing beyond the basics 1: Proven strategies professionals use to make their proposals work.* Portland, OR: Continuing Education Press, Portland State University.

Wells, M. K. (2005). *Grant writing beyond the basics 2: Understanding nonprofit finances.* Portland, OR: Continuing Education Press, Portland State University.

Wells, M. K. (2007). *Grant writing beyond the basics 3: Successful program evaluation.* Portland, OR: Continuing Education Press, Portland State University.

Index

I

identity, 3, 5, 39, 85, 102, 106

impact, 13, 17, 21, 35, 38, 69, 70, 72, 76, 77, 83, 85, 86, 87, 88, 90, 92, 94, 97, 107, 113, 117

implementation, 2, 34, 38, 39, 45, 57, 61, 80, 88, 93, 100

inductive, 4, 20, 24, 41, 52, 53, 60, 108

Inductive logic, 52, 53

industry, 10, 35, 45, 46, 48, 49, 65, 71, 72, 73, 77, 78, 79, 88, 91, 103, 104, 110

in-kind, 34, 35

innovative, 1, 27, 48, 50, 56, 88, 92

Inquiry, 49

intellectual property management, 87

internships, 30

investigator, 9, 19, 30, 45, 73, 82, 89, 90, 91, 99, 100, 114

IRB, 88, 89

J

jargon, 59, 66

K

key, 2, 5, 6, 8, 9, 16, 20, 22, 24, 25, 26, 28, 34, 40, 50, 58, 74, 75, 76, 84, 89, 90, 93, 94, 99, 100, 104, 109, 113

L

Lessons, xiii, xiv, 82, 108

licensing, 87

limitations, 15

literature, 4, 13, 14, 20, 26, 47, 52, 56, 93, 107, 112

local, 9, 13, 30, 32, 33, 34, 35, 44, 48, 57, 61, 65, 70, 71, 73, 74, 76, 78, 80, 88, 95, 98, 104, 105, 106, 107

logic, 4, 20, 21, 23, 24, 25, 36, 41, 52, 53, 108

LOI, 75, 104

praise, 43, 66

pre-correct, 9, 16, 43, 68, 92

premises, xv, 4, 24, 50, 51, 52, 53, 58, 59, 61, 62, 63

Principles, xii, xv, 4, 11, 48, 117

priority, 14, 15, 21, 45, 49, 51, 55, 61

private, xi, 2, 11, 12, 13, 14, 15, 19, 25, 32, 33, 34, 35, 36, 44, 53, 57, 65, 66, 70, 71, 73,
74, 75, 80, 82, 86, 95, 98, 102, 103, 104, 105, 106, 107

problem, 14, 15, 21, 24, 44, 48, 50, 51, 55, 56, 57, 67, 79, 83, 94

products, 15, 17, 46, 78, 79, 80, 87, 92

professionals, 1, 2, 6, 9, 15, 23, 28, 30, 32, 65, 66, 73, 77, 79, 86, 92, 94, 100, 118

profile, x, 5, 16, 23, 37

program, 5, 10, 33, 34, 39, 45, 47, 49, 57, 59, 70, 77, 78, 92, 103, 106, 107, 118

progress, 17, 33, 41, 44, 73, 93, 95

project, 5, 6, 11, 13, 17, 19, 27, 29, 33, 34, 35, 36, 39, 42, 45, 66, 68, 69, 73, 74, 75, 79, 86,
88, 100, 101, 106, 107, 110

proposals, v, 3, 4, 5, 6, 9, 10, 11, 12, 13, 14, 19, 22, 27, 29, 30, 32, 34, 37, 38, 39, 40, 41,
42, 43, 44, 48, 50, 55, 57, 65, 66, 68, 69, 70, 71, 73, 75, 76, 77, 80, 81, 83, 84, 90, 91,
93, 96, 97, 98, 103, 105, 106, 109, 110, 118

publish, 72, 75

R

random, 76, 88

redundancy, xv, 28, 54, 63

rejected, vi, 11, 34, 44, 45, 68, 71, 82, 92, 97, 100, 109

relationships, 6, 46, 47, 48, 59, 71, 77, 78, 79, 89, 101, 102, 104, 105, 106, 107

relevance, 14, 27, 41, 49, 56, 74, 83, 86

reporting, 5, 6, 34, 35, 38, 71, 106

resiliency, 39

resources, 1, 29, 45, 76, 82, 99, 100, 112

resubmissions, 13, 73, 103

resume, 69

review panel, 9, 65, 66, 69, 70, 72, 82, 87, 104, 105

reviewers, 5, 9, 16, 17, 20, 22, 27, 28, 29, 31, 33, 34, 36, 40, 43, 44, 45, 50, 54, 55, 64, 65,
66, 67, 68, 69, 82, 84, 86, 87, 92, 94, 96, 98, 99, 100, 102, 108

RFP, 19, 31, 32, 33, 47, 73, 74, 75, 80, 84, 97, 100, 104, 109 risks, 28, 38, 71, 106

rubric, 20, 44

rule, 3, 9, 12, 14, 20, 21, 31, 32, 33, 34, 35, 45, 50, 52, 53, 62, 65, 66, 68, 69, 75, 82, 92, 94, 98, 99, 100, 103

S

sacrifice, 17

salaries, 33, 35, 114, 116

scenarios, 68, 70

Schema, 20

Schemata, 20, 21

scope of work, 13

scored, 66, 83, 84, 87, 94, 96

seminars, 75

Simile, 60

skill set, 6, 8, 11, 29, 38, 39

skills, x, 1, 2, 3, 6, 8, 10, 11, 16, 19, 23, 24, 28, 29, 36, 38, 40, 43, 49, 61, 74, 77, 79, 96, 104, 109, 110

social, 2, 37, 43, 46, 55, 57, 74, 77, 87, 88

solution, 14, 15, 21, 56, 57, 67

solutions, 7, 14, 15, 42, 43, 48, 49, 55, 56, 103, 109

stage, 76, 77

stakeholders, 35, 70, 75, 79, 105, 107

standard, 23, 54, 62, 80, 85, 89, 98

state funding, 11, 102

statistical, 74, 86, 104

Story Telling, xii, 31

storyteller, 14, 104

strategy, xv, 9, 19, 20, 22, 55, 63, 67, 68, 69, 75, 79, 88, 89

structure, 5, 15, 21, 26, 33, 39, 58, 76, 91

sustainable, 78, 105

systematically, 14, 17, 67

systemic, iii, v, xv, 5, 6, 10, 11, 16, 37, 65, 111

www.ingramcontent.com/pod-product-compliance
Lightning Source LLC
Chambersburg PA
CBHW050349280326
41933CB00010BA/1395